RELIGIOUS STUDIES for
COMMON ENTRANCE
SECOND EDITION

**THE
HARRODIAN SCHOOL**

Year book purchased: JUL 2014

YEAR	PUPIL	FORM	CONDITION

This edition is dedicated to colleagues and pupils at St Hugh's School, and also to my nephew Robert Madeley and nieces Hannah and Alice Nanton who use this book.

The author

Susan Grenfell graduated from Oxford University with a Bachelor of Education degree in Theology. She taught Religious Studies at Caldicott Preparatory School and was Head of Study Skills and Learning Support there. She is now Head of Religious Education at St Hugh's Preparatory School, Faringdon. She has been on the executive committee for the Independent Schools Religious Studies Association for the past three years. She also runs Study Skills courses at prep schools.

Advisers

The author and publisher would like to thank Michael Wilcockson for his support and advice during the writing stage, and for his valuable contribution to the standards and marking guides for Common Entrance examinations.

The author and publisher would also like to thank Ann Meisner, Olie Bullock and Jennie Williams for their valuable contribution to this book.

All Bible quotations are taken from The New International Version, the recommended text for Common Entrance. See page 164 for further details.

Words printed in SMALL CAPITALS (first mention only) are defined in the Glossary on pages 160–161.

Although every effort has been made to ensure that website addresses are correct at time of going to press, Hodder Education cannot be held responsible for the content of any website mentioned in this book.

Orders: please contact Bookpoint Ltd, 130 Milton Park, Abingdon, Oxon OX14 4SB. Telephone: +44 (0)1235 827720. Fax: +44 (0)1235 400454. Lines are open from 9.00a.m. to 6.00p.m., Monday to Saturday, with a 24-hour message answering service. Visit our website at www.hoddereducation.co.uk

© Susan Grenfell 2006, 2011

First published in 2006

This second edition published in 2011
by Hodder Education,
an Hachette UK company
338 Euston Road
London NW1 3BH

Impression number	5 4
Year	2015 2014 2013

Original layouts by Fiona Webb
Artwork by Oxford Designers & Illustrators Ltd, Jon Davis and Phil Garner
Typeset in Boton Light 12pt by Fakenham Prepress Solutions, Fakenham, Norfolk NR21 8NN
Printed in Dubai

A catalogue record for this title is available from the British Library

ISBN 978 1 444 12425 5

Teacher's Resource Book second edition ISBN 978 1 444 12426 2

RELIGIOUS STUDIES for
COMMON ENTRANCE

SECOND EDITION

SUSAN GRENFELL

HODDER
EDUCATION
AN HACHETTE UK COMPANY

Contents

Introduction to the Bible

What is the Bible?

The Bible is a kind of library; it is made up of many different books. It is divided into two sections: the OLD TESTAMENT and the NEW TESTAMENT. The word 'testament' means COVENANT or agreement. So the Old Testament is about the old covenant that God had with humankind, which he drew up with Moses. The New Testament is about the new covenant, which was introduced by Jesus. Jews **and** Christians believe that the Old Testament is the word of God. Only Christians believe that the New Testament is the word of God.

How to look things up in the Bible

The Bible is divided into books, the names of which are often shortened, for example Gen for Genesis. Each book is divided into chapters and verses. The chapter numbers appear at the top of each page in the Bible and are in bold in the text. The verses are numbered in the text.

Pentateuch or Torah

The first five books of the Bible are called the Pentateuch – *penta* means 'five' in Latin. These books make up the Jewish *Torah*, which means 'Law'. By obeying the Law, the Israelite people kept their side of the covenant and, in return, God protected them. The Law covered all areas of life from what food to eat to commands such as not to murder. The Law is summed up in the Ten Commandments.

History

These books record the history of the Jewish people in Canaan, their time in exile and their return to Israel. The books reveal the achievements and failures of Israel's kings and commanders. It records the nation's constant departures from following God, and their times of REPENTANCE and return to worshipping him.

Poetry and wisdom literature

King Solomon's reign was a time when learning was encouraged. Poetry was written. People made pilgrimages – special journeys to WORSHIP in a HOLY place. They went to Jerusalem because it was where Solomon had built the TEMPLE. Psalms were sung on the way, a bit like the way you sing songs on the school bus going to matches. Wisdom literature gives common sense advice from a spiritual point of view.

Prophets

There were two kinds of PROPHET in the Old Testament: political prophets like Elijah, and SPIRITUAL prophets like Amos. A prophet acted as a middle man between God and humans. He took the requests of the people to God and told the people what God required of them.
The books also contain prophetic passages – foretelling the future – about the coming of a MESSIAH.

Gospels

The Gospels record the life and teaching of Jesus. The word GOSPEL means 'good news'.

Acts of the Apostles

The book of Acts takes the story of the Gospels further and charts the beginning of Christianity and its spread throughout the Mediterranean world.

Letters to the churches

The letters are from early CHRISTIAN leaders to the CHURCHES they started on their MISSIONARY journeys. The letters teach much of what now makes up guidelines for Christian living.

The book of Revelation is not actually a letter. It is a unique book full of prophecies and visions and was written by a man called John.

⚫⚫ Think and write ...

1 Why is 'library' a good description of the Bible?
2 Write a sentence to explain what these words mean:
   a) Torah   **b)** Pentateuch   **c)** Testament
   d) Prophet   **e)** Gospel.
3 Why do you think there are two Testaments?
4 Copy this chart and complete it. Each section has been started for you using the shortened forms.

Section	Contents
The Torah	Gen. Ex. Lev ...
The History of the Jews	Josh. Judges, Ruth ...
Wisdom Literature	Ps ...
The Prophets	Is. Jer. Lam. Ez ...
Gospels	Matt ...
Acts	
Letters	Rom. 1 & 2 Cor ...

encounter

● ● Starter

Discuss a time when you made something that you were pleased with or disappointed with.

The story of the Creation in **Genesis 1** is one of the most famous parts of the Bible – you may think you know it already. You can read the whole text in your Bible, but here is an overview of the big ideas.

In the beginning God created the universe:

...day and night...

...sea and sky...

...land, plants and trees...

DAY 4

...Sun and Moon...

DAY 5

...fish and birds...

DAY 6

...animals and human beings...

DAY 7

... God rested.

. . . and God saw that it was good.

Now read **Genesis 2** for another version of how it all started. Notice the detail with which the writer describes the creation of the man and the woman. See how he places the emphasis on human beings and how everything that was created was made for their use.

● ● **Think and write ...**

1 Make a pie chart to show the six days of Creation and what was created on each.
2 Do you think days off are important? Why? What do you do on your days off?

● ● **Digging deeper**

3 Why do you think God was pleased with what he saw?
4 Would he feel the same way now? Give reasons for your answer.

The Creation

△ Why do human beings like the company of others?

● ● Discuss

In Genesis 1, verse 26 the writer says human beings were 'in God's likeness' or 'like God'. What do you think the writer meant? That they had:
● power over animals, fish, birds and the environment
● creative ability to design and make things
● ability to think and make decisions
● knowledge of the difference between good and evil (Genesis 3, Unit 2 page 12)?
Explain your answer.

●●● **Activity**

1 Imagine God is making another world. How would you advise him? In groups, make a list of five things you would like to stay the same as this world and five things that you would like to be different.

Humans

The writer of the first Creation story is referred to by theologians as 'P'. P says in verse 26 that humans were created in God's likeness. This means that they share God's characteristics. For example human beings have power and can create things of beauty, show mercy, care about justice and can demonstrate great love and compassion. These qualities set humans apart from animals. God made them stewards, responsible for looking after the world for him.

God

The Creation stories reveal a majestic and powerful God. His authority lay in the BELIEF that he had designed and created the world, therefore he was responsible for it. The whole of Creation, including humans, was answerable to him.

It was good

Notice that at the end of each 'day' God pronounces what he has made as 'good'. The writer was making the point that at the beginning, everything was perfect. The concepts of shame and guilt, which enter the story of the Bible in the next unit, are not mentioned in the Creation accounts. Nakedness was a symbol of shame in early cultures and the last verse in the chapter specifically says that the man and woman were 'naked but not ashamed'. They had not yet encountered evil.

●● **Think and write ...**

2 Why did people want to write down stories about the Creation?
3 Write down three main differences between the two Creation stories in Genesis 1 and 2.

Rest

Day seven is the Sabbath and is the name used by the Jews for the day of rest. God had worked at creation and now he rested, secure in the knowledge that what he had created was perfect.

Two stories

Having two Creation stories adds to the richness of the Biblical accounts of how things began. The second story adds to the first:

● the idea of God creating a beautiful garden, called the Garden of Eden, in which humans can live. The garden had everything needed to keep them alive: fruit, water, fish, birds and game. God even provided gold and precious stones (Genesis 2.12).

● the idea of humans naming everything. Naming in Eastern culture is part of having authority over that thing or person.

●● **Digging deeper**

4 Make a list of the responsibilities God gave humans.
5 What insights does the writer of the second Creation story have about human nature?

● the idea of limits within life. God planted the Tree of Life and the Tree of Knowledge. God told humans that they were not to eat the fruit of the Tree of Knowledge.

● the idea that humans need company. Man and woman were made for each other – for working together, for friendship and for having children. These mirror the ideals of marriage set out in Genesis 2.24.

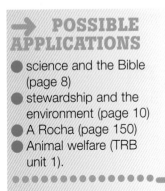

→ **POSSIBLE APPLICATIONS**

● science and the Bible (page 8)
● stewardship and the environment (page 10)
● A Rocha (page 150)
● Animal welfare (TRB unit 1).

Science and the Bible

Some people may find it odd that the opening pages of the Bible describe how the world and human beings were created. But people have always asked about where they came from, and cultures all over the world have their own creation stories. Around 500 BCE, the traditions of the Jews began to be written down. The writers started from the belief that God created the world.

Science looks for evidence, from which the underlying laws of nature can be worked out. Evidence can be gained from experiments, such as those you do in science lessons. Evidence can also be found everywhere in the world. For instance, people have found very old fossils that come from animals, such as dinosaurs, which are no longer on Earth.

Two theories scientists use today

The **Big Bang Theory** describes how the universe began. It is based on Edwin Hubble's discovery in the 1920s that the further a galaxy is from us the faster it moves away. About 14 thousand million years ago the universe came into being by exploding outwards from an incredibly hot and dense space much smaller than the full stop at the end of this sentence.

The **Theory of Evolution** describes how life arose on Earth and is based largely on the work of Charles Darwin. Very simple organisms gradually changed and became more complex, producing plants, then animals, and finally, more intelligent life such as humans. Fossils provide much of the evidence for evolution.

△ This fossil was found in America and is about 50 million years old.

These theories, and others, do not agree with the account at the beginning of Genesis, which says that God created the Earth and all life on it in six days. Many take this as proof that the Bible is wrong and that science shows God does not exist. Others argue that the scientific and religious accounts can co-exist; many scientists are Christians.

The story of Galileo

By studying the planets, Galileo became convinced that the Earth went round the Sun and not the other way round. The Church leaders were angry because they believed that the Bible said the Sun went round the Earth.

Has science disproved God?

God of the Gaps

In the past, people thought God actively intervened to keep the universe working properly, making the Sun rise, the seasons come and go, and the rain fall. This argument is called the 'God of the Gaps' because it uses God to fill the gaps in our current understanding. We now understand about the rotation of the Earth and the water cycle. If, one day, science can explain everything, so the argument goes, we shall not need God at all.

The Creationist view

● Creationists are Christians who believe that the Bible is true in every detail: everything was created by God in six days of 24 hours each. They say that science is not as accurate as is often made out and contains serious errors, one of which they claim is the Theory of Evolution. Creationists argue that fossils were created like everything else, in the first week, and that humans and dinosaurs must have existed together. They believe that the dinosaurs died out in the Flood at the time of Noah.

● Creationists also believe that the world is quite young. An important scholar called James Ussher who lived in the 17th century, used the genealogies in the Bible to calculate when creation happened. He arrived at the date 4004 BC, making the earth about 6000 years old. This disagrees with modern science which says that it is thousands of millions of years old.

● Creationists say that either the Bible is true or science is, but you cannot believe both.

A moderate Christian view

● Most Christians say that we should not read the Bible as scientific fact. The writer of Genesis is saying that God created the world and everything in it, and the days represent stages in the world's development, not 24-hour periods. The Bible tells us that God **did** create the world, and science tells us **how**. In this way science and religion complement each other.

● There is no evidence in nature that he does not exist.

● The story is timeless and can speak to anyone no matter where they live or how little education they have received.

A Humanist view

The world described by science is all there is. There is no God behind the scenes. Because science works with what can be observed and measured, it has nothing to say about God.

●●● **Activity**

1 In groups, make a poster of:
Either all the reasons you can think of that might point to the existence of God.
Or all the reasons you can think of that might place doubt on the existence of God.
2 How is this exercise unlike a scientific experiment?

●● **Think and write ...**

3 What do Creationists believe?
4 How is this different from a moderate Christian view?

●● **Digging deeper**

5 Genesis says that the world was created in six days; science says it took millions of years.
Can they both be right? Give reasons for your answer.

Stewardship and the environment

● ● Discuss

a) Do you think humans have the right to use the Earth's resources as they wish?

b) What rights do animals have?

Genesis 1.28 says, 'Rule over the fish in the sea and the birds in the sky and over every living creature that moves on the ground.'

Over the centuries, most people have acted as if they can do anything they like with the Earth's resources, including all wildlife. For centuries this attitude has had little global effect, although animals have become extinct through excessive hunting.

Other people, especially in the last 30 years, have thought more about what being a good steward means. They say that STEWARDSHIP is about looking after the world, not exploiting it. Being a steward means looking after something for someone else, usually the person to whom it belongs. Christians believe the world belongs to God. However, the world is also there for future generations to enjoy.

Many Christians now believe they should be actively involved in conservation because this is in obedience to God's command. They are beginning to understand why there was such a command in the first place. A good example of a charity that began work in conservation for just this reason, is 'A Rocha', which you can read about in section 3 of this book. They have projects in many parts of the world and encourage people to support their work. They want to make the natural world a better place to live in.

What has changed?

● Over-fishing and over-hunting have led to the extinction of some species; others are at risk.

● Cutting down the rainforests for building, cultivation and roads (see picture A). Animals and birds are losing their natural habitats and scientists are worried about the effect on the balance of nature.

● Burning fossil fuels (see picture B) has created what is called the greenhouse effect. As the temperature of the Earth rises, the climate is affected. Already Britain is experiencing freak weather conditions, and hurricanes and tornadoes are devastating parts of the world. New Orleans suffered appalling damage and loss when Hurricane Katrina struck the city in 2005. More recently in 2008, the Republic of Haiti was hit by storms and devastated by flooding. 2010 saw some of the worst floods in Pakistan where whole regions were left uninhabitable.

● Polluting the environment, for example:

The use of CFCs has damaged the ozone layer. This has led to an increase in skin cancers.

Acid rain is killing trees and plants, and poisoning rivers.

Industrial waste pollutes rivers, seas, land and air.

Accidents involving oil tankers cause massive oil spills that pollute the coastline and sea life. In 2010 a BP oil pipe ruptured off the coast of America causing extensive damage to marine life.

understand

apply 2

△ Huge areas of forest are cut down and burned every day to make way for cultivated land. This photo shows deforestation for manganese mining activities in Brazil.

△ Smoke billows from the chimneys of China's largest iron and steel works.

What can be done to prevent more damage being done?

Environmental groups can put pressure on companies and governments they think are damaging our world. They also arrange holidays where people can do conservation in a particular area.

CONSERVATION
DOING SOMETHING
THE ENVIRONMENT
TO HELP

Individuals can join one of the environmental organisations or raise money for them. They can write to their MPs about environmental issues that worry them. They can recycle their rubbish.

Governments can raise environmental issues in meetings with other world leaders. They can get together to set targets to reduce pollution. For example, more countries than ever before came together in Copenhagen in December 2009 to agree measures for reducing climate change. It is important for an agreement to be in place before the terms of the environmental treaty made in Kyoto come to an end in 2012.

●● **Think and write ...**

1 Write a sentence to explain what pollution is.
2 What does the term 'stewardship' mean?
3 How can you as an individual be a 'good steward'? Write a word or phrase to represent your idea on a balloon, then blow it up. Make a class display.
4 How can governments influence global warming?
5 How can organisations such as Friends of the Earth and Greenpeace help control damage to the environment?

●● **Digging deeper**

6 'I am only one person. I can't possibly make a difference.' What would you say to someone who held that view?

2 The nature of humanity and the Fall

encounter

● ● Starter

Discuss what you think it means to be 'only human'.

Scene is set in the Garden of Eden.

Serpent: SSSSSSSSSSSSS

Eve: *(startled)* Oh, you made me jump!

Serpent: Nice set-up you've got here.

Eve: We think so.

Serpent: Getting on all right with God then, are you?

Eve: We have everything we could possibly want.

Serpent: Well, you would say that, wouldn't you? Being loyal and that.

Eve: *(puzzled)* What do you mean?

Serpent: *(gesturing to the trees around them)* Let you eat all the fruit, does he?

Eve: Yes, nearly all. What are you getting at?

Serpent: Aha! I knew it! He's keeping something from you – and you don't even know what it is, do you? *(disgustedly)* And you let him.

Eve: *(defensively)* He said we could eat any fruit we liked except the fruit on that tree, over there in the middle.

Serpent: Looks sweet though, don't you think? Go on, you must have tried it.

Eve: He said we'd die if we so much as touched it.

Serpent: And you believed him? What a sucker! You won't die. Want to know why God really told you not to eat it?

Eve: *(uncertainly)* Why?

Serpent: Because he knows that if you do, you'll be wise like him, you will know good and you will know evil – that's why.

Eve: Oh, I see. Well, it does look tasty I must say. Delicously juicy in fact. *(wistfully)* It would be nice to be wise; not that I'm not clever or anything you understand . . . just wiser, you know . . . it would be wonderful to be really wise.

Serpent: I would go for it if I were you, while you've got the chance. Then you can wow that husband of yours.

Eve: I think I will. *(picks some fruit and eats it)* Hmmmmmmm!

Serpent: Ha ha ha ha ha *(slithers away chortling to himself)*

Enter Adam

Eve: *(holding out the fruit)* Try some. I met this snake creature just now and he told me the real reason we aren't allowed to eat the fruit off that tree.

Adam: Oh yeah? What's that then?

Eve: God's afraid we'll become like him, you know, knowing everything.

Adam: I'm not sure that's such a good idea, Eve. What's wrong with the way things are now? Everything's perfect. Why, have you just eaten some?

Eve: Yes.

Adam: And you're not dead or anything?

Eve: Do I look dead?

Adam: Er . . . no.

Eve: Go on, have some yourself.

Adam: We-ell . . . I don't know . . . OK then. *(Adam eats some)*

Eve: Well? How do you feel? Has it worked?

Adam: Actually, I'm not sure. I don't know what I feel. I feel different; maybe because

things are in sharp focus where before they were a bit blurred. I guess that's being wise or something. But there're other thoughts coming too . . . I mean, I feel ashamed that we have done something we shouldn't have. It's made me feel naked.

Eve: Me too.

Adam: Perhaps we'll feel better if we're properly dressed. Fig leaves will do for a start; how many do you think we'll need?

Later that evening

God: Adam! Eve?

Adam: *(stage whisper)* Oh no, that's God! Quick, hide! Don't let him see us like this.

Eve: What shall we do? I wish I'd never eaten that rotten old fruit. I've had a horrid feeling all day.

Adam: It's your own fault. And you made me eat some. Nothing's the same any more. Everything's spoilt.

God: Hey guys! Where are you? This isn't like you!

Adam: *(coming out from behind a tree)* We're here. We heard you in the garden.

God: Well, naturally. I often come here. Where's Eve?

Eve: I'm here.

Adam: We hid because we were afraid.

God: I can see that. What are those things you're wearing? Who told you to do that?

Adam: Well . . . we were ashamed. I mean . . . we felt we should . . . you know . . . be dressed.

God: *(with an edge to his voice)* You've gone and done it, haven't you? Eaten the fruit I told you not to eat?

Adam: It wasn't my fault. It's all the fault of that woman you put here with me. She egged me on to eat it. Blame her!

God: *(to Eve)* Well? Why did you do this?

Eve: It wasn't my fault either. That snake tricked me into eating it. *(outraged)* He lied to me!

Serpent: O–oh!

God: *(wrathfully)* You will be punished for doing this. Out of all the animals, you will be cursed. You will crawl on your belly and eat dust. You will no longer be safe from people, nor will they be safe from you. They will crush your head and you will bite their heels.

Serpent slinks away hissing softly

God: Eve . . . you must face the consequences of your disobedience. You want to know what it's like being God? Did you think Creation was a piece of cake? No . . . creation can be painful as you will find out when you have children. And don't think you can avoid it, because wanting them is part of your genetic make-up. Because you are weaker than Adam, you and all women after you will have to be subject to men.

Adam: That's an excellent idea if you don't mind my saying so . . .

God: *(interrupting)* And you! You also disobeyed me. You should never have listened to your wife when she tried to make you do wrong. See this ground? Never given you much trouble before, has it? Well it will from now on . . . when you have to dig it. You will work all your life to make this dusty ground grow food for you and your family. It will produce weeds and thorns, which will add to your difficulties.

Adam: That is so unfair . . .

God: Stop moaning, I haven't finished yet. You wanted to be like me. You should never have believed the snake; he's a liar. Yes, you will know the difference between good and evil, but there was one little detail he left out. You now know that you are mortal and you will die, not today, not tomorrow, but sometime. You will become dust just like the soil.

Read the complete story in **Genesis 3**.

⬤ ⬤ Think and write . . .

1 What aspects of human nature did Adam and Eve show in the story?
2 What were the consequences of Adam and Eve's disobedience?
3 What persuasive arguments did the serpent use to tempt Eve?

The nature of humanity and the Fall

The Garden of Eden

The word 'Eden' means 'delight'. The Greek word for garden translates as 'paradise' or parkland. Eden is described in Genesis as being somewhere between the Rivers Tigris and Euphrates, in what is now Iraq and Iran. The picture is painted of God and people living and working harmoniously together.

The Tree of Knowledge

There are many theories as to what the fruit of this tree represents but the importance of the tree lies in the fact that it was forbidden. It offered an alternative to obedience to God. It offered people the opportunity to become 'self-made', having to extract knowledge, values and satisfaction from the world by themselves. The word 'knowledge' might be better translated as 'experience'. Philip Pullman calls it 'Dust' in the *His Dark Materials* trilogy.

The Serpent

The camouflaged, sinuous serpent makes a perfect symbol for the devil. In this story, he deceives Eve into thinking it is safe and in her best interests to eat the fruit. (Look at the story and see how he does it. Many of our television advertisements use the same tactics.) Another way of thinking about the serpent is to think of it as symbolising our bad selves.

The Act

Eve made her own decision about whether or not to eat the fruit. She listened to the tempter, looked at the fruit, picked it and ate it. At any time during this process, she could have said 'no'. She did not and life was never the same again. Worse was to come as she successfully tempted Adam to eat some too. Adam did not have the strength of mind to refuse her.

The Consequences

◁ *Man being expelled from the Garden*, a painting by He Qi.

understand

The Results

In Old Testament days, nakedness was a symbol of shame and that is why they were concerned to cover themselves up. They had been sold a false idea of evil as something wise and sophisticated that would bring greatness, when it was just greed. They had been duped. They looked at the familiar world and it was spoilt. They also knew that they could not face God. This was the main consequence of their disobedience or SIN as the Bible calls it. Sin cuts people off from God. It is worth noting here that the main theme of the Bible is how God tries to reverse this situation – more of that later.

- The serpent's punishment was humiliation – to be trampled on. There would also be a constant battle (enmity) between good and evil with people trying to do what is right but tempted to do what is wrong. Some theologians say this is what it means when it says 'I will put enmity between you and the woman, and between your offspring and hers.' (verse 15)
- The woman's punishment was to know (experience) suffering. Childbirth is the most fundamental human process but it is painful. The other bit of bad news for Eve was that man and woman would not feel equal any more. The man would exert his authority over the woman.
- The man's punishment was to sweat and toil to survive.

The place of this story in the Bible and its relevance today

All religions attempt to answer the problem of evil and suffering in the world and they nearly all attribute it to wrongdoing or 'sin' on the part of human beings. The clash between good and evil is worldwide as people struggle within themselves to do what is right and resist what is wrong. Whether you take the story in Genesis literally or symbolically, it paints a picture of a good thing gone bad because of something people did. The theme of SALVATION, which runs through the Bible, starts here and ends with the CRUCIFIXION and RESURRECTION of Jesus.

●● Discuss

a) Later interpretations of the story in the Bible teach that human beings are all born with 'fallen' (sinful) natures. That means that everyone is predisposed to do wrong.

   The poet William Wordsworth, on the other hand, described children as being born 'trailing clouds of glory'. He meant that people are born good.
   i) What do you think? Are children born sinful or good?
   ii) Can you remember the first naughty things you did?
   iii) Is childish naughtiness the same as sin?

b) If you learn something, you cannot un-learn it. Is knowledge always a good thing?

c) Why do we read the story of the Fall at Christmas?

●● Think and write …

1 Study picture A. Describe the mood and feelings of each character: the angel, Adam and Eve.
2 What is sin?
3 What does the Tree of Knowledge symbolise?
4 Explain Adam's and Eve's feelings after they had eaten the fruit.
5 How might one see the punishments as consequences of their actions?

→ **POSSIBLE APPLICATIONS**
- consequences (page 16)
- giving in to temptation (page 90).

Talk about a time when someone spoilt what would otherwise have been a perfect day or a beautiful place.

Consequences

1

VANDALS BREAK IN AT THE ANGUS CAIRNS PREPARATORY SCHOOL

Vandals broke into the Angus Cairns Prep School last night and wrecked the new Performing Arts Centre, just one day before it was due to be opened by the Chairman of Governors, Sir Anthony Richards.

The centre, which cost over two million pounds to build, was completed in the summer and pupils were looking forward to using it in September.

The vandals gained access to the building by throwing a large rock through one of the windows. The rock damaged a wall inside.

Police reported that four computers were stolen and the stage lighting system destroyed. Spray paint cans had been used on the walls of the main hall and two of the classrooms. In the basement cloakrooms, taps had been left on and basins pulled out from the wall.

Pupils arriving at the school for the beginning of the new term stared in disbelief at the wanton destruction all around them.

Sarah Mayhew, aged 12, said that she was shocked by what she saw. 'Everyone worked very hard to raise the money for this centre,' she said. 'Now it's all spoilt. We were going to do a performance of *Oliver!* this term, to open it properly. I don't see how we can do it now.'

Tom Porter, the head boy, also condemned the vandalism. 'They shouldn't be allowed to get away with it,' he said.

Asked how he felt about the damaged hall, the headmaster said, 'Naturally I am upset. This is an act of mindless vandalism and everyone will be very disappointed not to be able to use the new centre they've worked so hard for.'

2

George's story

George was feeling wretched. After what he had done, would his father ever trust him again? Gone was the easy relationship they had had, and replacing it was a nasty sort of polite distance. If only he hadn't lied about watching that DVD; if only he hadn't watched it full stop! He knew he wasn't allowed to watch adult films, but everyone else at school seemed to have seen this one. Why was his dad so stuffy? George had tried to explain that Matt had encouraged him to watch it. Matt was his older brother and now he was in trouble too and Matt was furious with George for involving him.

Now he faced a weekend of boredom. Not only was he not allowed to see his friends, but his father wasn't going to take him to the match either. They had such good times together on a Saturday and now it was spoilt. He thought back to what his father had said. 'George, this isn't only about doing something your mother and I have told you not to do. It's about not telling the truth. Lying gets in the way of a happy relationship.'

Well, that was certainly true. George didn't feel happy at all, and it was because he had disobeyed his parents and he didn't like the consequences.

●● Think and write . . .

Read the newspaper article (story 1) and George's story (story 2). In each case something good has been spoilt.
1 Write down what had been good in each case.
2 Write down what spoiled it.
3 How are both these stories a bit like the story of Adam and Eve in this unit?

●● Digging deeper

4 Is it harder to accept consequences caused by our own bad behaviour than those caused by other people's bad behaviour? Give reasons for your answer.

encounter

understand

●● Starter

●● **Starter**

Discuss: what kind of things make you jealous?

The story of Cain's jealousy of his brother Abel ended in murder. You can read the whole story in **Genesis 4.1–16**.

ADAM AND EVE SLEPT TOGETHER. EVE BECAME PREGNANT AND GAVE BIRTH TO A SON, CALLED CAIN.

LATER SHE HAD ANOTHER SON, ABEL.

CAIN GREW UP TO WORK THE SOIL; ABEL BECAME A SHEPHERD.

IN TIME, CAIN BROUGHT SOME OF HIS HARVEST AS AN OFFERING TO GOD. ABEL BROUGHT THE BEST LAMB OF HIS FLOCK.

GOD WAS PLEASED WITH ABEL'S OFFERING, BUT NOT WITH CAIN'S. ABEL WAS A GOOD MAN, A MAN OF FAITH, BUT GOD COULD SEE THE DARKNESS IN CAIN'S HEART.

AND SO GOD SAID:

BUT CAIN REFUSED TO LISTEN TO GOD. HE BURNED WITH RAGE.

CAIN WAS FURIOUS.

WHY SO ANGRY, CAIN? NO NEED TO SCOWL IF YOU HAVE DONE RIGHT.

IF NOT, SIN IS CROUCHING BY THE DOOR OF YOUR LIFE. IT WANTS TO CONTROL YOU.

BUT YOU MUST FIGHT IT!

ALLOWING HIS ANGER TO RULE HIM, HE PLOTTED AGAINST HIS BROTHER...

1 Make a list of the events that led up to Cain becoming a nomad.
2 Look up Genesis 4.3–4. Both brothers offered a SACRIFICE. Look very carefully at what they gave.
   a) Which two adjectives are missing in the description of what Cain offered?
   b) What does that tell you about their characters, especially their attitude to their God?
3 Draw an outline of a man and label him 'Cain'. On one side, write in green pen what Cain thought and felt. On the other side, write in red pen what he did.

Cain and Abel

Adam and Eve were no longer living in the Garden of Eden. They had to farm the land. Their two sons, Cain and Abel, had different but equally important jobs. Cain was a farmer and grew crops, vegetables and fruit for the family, while Abel looked after the sheep. Life was precarious in those days and it was the custom to make offerings to God. This was to show gratitude for his provision, and to ask for his protection against bad things happening. Only the best was good enough for such offerings, so Abel gave the pick of the flock and Cain offered some of the grain. Abel's sacrifice was pleasing to the Lord, but Cain's was rejected.

Why did God reject Cain's sacrifice?

It seems on the surface to be rather unfair.

Anyone who studies other stories in the Bible will quickly see that God always looks at the heart – at motives and character – before looking at the action.

Verses 5 and 6 give a clue because they reveal Cain as an angry young man. He had a violent temper. The text says he became 'very angry' because God rejected his sacrifice.

God pointed out that his anger was at the root of his problems and warned him that sin – which was probably the sin of anger – was waiting like a wild animal to overtake him.

GOD WAS PLEASED WITH ABEL'S OFFERING, BUT NOT WITH CAIN'S. ABEL WAS A GOOD MAN, A MAN OF FAITH, BUT GOD COULD SEE THE DARKNESS IN CAIN'S HEART.

CAIN WAS FURIOUS.

AND SO GOD SAID:

WHY SO ANGRY, CAIN ? NO NEED TO SCOWL IF YOU HAVE DONE RIGHT.

IF NOT, SIN IS CROUCHING BY THE DOOR OF YOUR LIFE. IT WANTS TO CONTROL YOU.

BUT YOU MUST FIGHT IT!

Why did Cain kill Abel?

Cain probably saw Abel as an annoying little brother, who had not only got the easier job of looking after the sheep – later, this became a job traditionally given to younger children – but who was preferred by God as well, which made Cain very jealous.

Unfortunately, he did not take any notice of God's warning about sin, and cold-bloodedly murdered Abel.

What happened next?

When God asked where Abel was, Cain answered like a moody teenager: 'How should I know? It's not my job to keep track of my brother all the time.'

God talked of Abel's blood calling to him from the ground. This is symbolic language meaning that God knew and cared that an innocent person had suffered at the hands of someone violent. Blood was a symbol of life.

What was God's judgement on Cain?

It is interesting that God did not strike Cain dead for what he had done. If you know Old Testament law, you might expect God to kill Cain. Instead he rehabilitated him. He sent him away from his family farm and the protection it offered him, into the no man's land around. Cain was terrified, so God put a protective mark on him to warn off wandering TRIBES who would have certainly killed him if they came across him.

During his remaining life, Cain would have the chance to try again. As God had expelled Adam and Eve from Eden (Unit 2), so he expelled their son from the farm but, as with Adam and Eve, he gave Cain a second chance.

●● Discuss

a) Anger is described as being like a wild animal crouching at the door, waiting to pounce and devour. How is this a good description of what happened to Cain?

b) What happens when a person becomes angry?

●● Think and write . . .

1 Why did people make offerings to God at this time?

2 Why do you think God accepted Abel's offering?

3 Draw a picture of an angry face. Around it, write down as many things as you can think of that might have made Cain angry.

4 Why does God say Abel's blood is 'crying out to me from the ground'?

5 What kind of life could Cain now expect to have?

●● Digging deeper

6 Explain why God rejected Cain's sacrifice.

7 Suggest at least two things Cain could have done to make his sacrifice acceptable.

8 What does the story tell us about God?

→ **POSSIBLE APPLICATIONS**
● dealing with anger and jealousy (page 22)
● punishment (page 46)
● reconciliation (page 146).

Dealing with anger and jealousy

If you have brothers and sisters, you will know that life isn't always easy. You live in the same house and share television, food, space, parental attention and possessions. This can lead to tensions that can cause jealousy and anger.

While we are at school, we live in a sort of extended family and we face situations there that can make us feel angry and jealous, just as Cain did. How we deal with them is a good test of our character.

● ● ● **Activity**

Use the 'Cain Scale' and find out how good you are at dealing with jealousy.

On your own copy of this questionnaire, tick only one box in answer to each of these questions. Total your score and find out where you are on the Cain Scale.

1 Your sister is given a larger helping of cake at tea. Do you:

  a) say nothing and eat your piece of cake ☐

  b) complain that she has taken the larger slice of cake and it's not fair ☐

  c) kick her shins under the table or knock against her deliberately? ☐

2 Your classmate is picked for the rugby/netball team and you aren't, even though you feel you are better than they are. Do you:

  a) pick a fight with them or say something spiteful about them to your friends ☐

  b) say 'They must be desperate if they picked you' ☐

  c) say 'Well done'? ☐

3 Your brother is given a new computer game and you aren't. Do you:

  a) scowl and demand unpleasantly to have a go ☐

  b) show interest and enthuse over it ☐

  c) thump him and take it off him so that you can have first go? ☐

4 A classmate is invited to a party and you aren't. Do you:

  a) tell them that you wouldn't go to that party if they paid you ☐

  b) say something horrible about the person whose party it is ☐

  c) help them decide what to wear, or think no more about it? ☐

5 Someone else gets chosen for the part in the play that you wanted, and you only get a walk-on part. Do you:

  a) congratulate them ☐

  b) hit them or hurt them in some way when no one is looking ☐

  c) say that you aren't going to take part in the play at all? ☐

understand

apply

6 Your friend's parents buy a really cool new car. Do you:

a) enthusiastically tell your parents about the new car ☐

b) go on and on to your dad about buying a new car ☐

c) kick the old car, the furniture, anything within kicking distance, as well as going on and on about a new car? ☐

7 Someone else gets their self-portrait put on the wall and the one you sweated over doesn't go up. Do you:

a) draw a moustache on the painting on the wall ☐

b) say something like 'Great painting' or shrug philosophically ☐

c) complain of unfairness and favouritism? ☐

8 Your not very bright classmate beats you in a Maths test. Do you:

a) cheat in the next Maths test so that you come top ☐

b) call them 'teacher's pet' or make some other derogatory remark ☐

c) say 'Well done'? ☐

9 Your best friend drops you and hangs about with someone else. Do you:

a) shrug and make other friends ☐

b) spread malicious rumours about them or pick a fight after school ☐

c) pointedly ignore both people? ☐

10 Your friend is made a prefect and you aren't. Do you:

a) congratulate them ☐

b) stop being friends with them ☐

c) refuse to co-operate and try to get them into trouble so that they lose their position? ☐

Scoring

1 a) 1 b) 2 c) 3	**6** a) 1 b) 2 c) 3
2 a) 3 b) 2 c) 1	**7** a) 3 b) 1 c) 2
3 a) 2 b) 1 c) 3	**8** a) 3 b) 2 c) 1
4 a) 2 b) 3 c) 1	**9** a) 1 b) 3 c) 2
5 a) 1 b) 3 c) 2	**10** a) 1 b) 2 c) 3

If you scored between 10 and 15 points

Your friends have nothing to fear. You value them more for who they are than what they have. Secrets, money, popularity – nothing is more important than friendship. You are self confident and usually generous with your praise.

If you scored between 16 and 23 points

You hold on to what's yours and although it hurts to see other people doing better than you or having more things than you, what can you do? *C'est la vie.* You might as well get used to it. Being unpleasant to others ultimately hurts you more than them.

If you scored over 23 points

Woe betide anyone who gets something you had your eye on! You allow your jealousy free rein and have probably been rather spoilt. You can be ruthless and calculating.

encounter

● ● Starter

Discuss:

1 What is your most treasured possession?

2 How would you feel if you had to give it up?

A ¹Some time later God tested Abraham. He said to him, 'Abraham!'

'Here I am!' he replied.

²Then God said, 'Take your son, your only son, Isaac, whom you love, and go to the region of Moriah. Sacrifice him there as a burnt offering on one of the mountains I will tell you about.'

³Early the next morning Abraham got up and saddled his donkey. He took with him two of his servants and his son Isaac. When he had cut enough wood for the burnt offering, he set out for the place God had told him about. ⁴On the third day Abraham looked up and saw the place in the distance. ⁵He said to his servants, 'Stay here with the donkey while I and the boy go over there. We will worship and then we will come back to you.'

⁶Abraham took the wood for the burnt offering and placed it on his son Isaac, and he himself carried the fire and the knife. As the two of them went on together, ⁷Isaac spoke up and said to his father Abraham, 'Father?'

'Yes, my son?' Abraham replied.

'The fire and wood are here,' Isaac said, 'but where is the lamb for the burnt offering?'

⁸Abraham answered, 'God himself will provide the lamb for the burnt offering, my son.' And the two of them went on together.

⁹When they reached the place God had told him about, Abraham built an altar there and arranged the wood on it. He bound his son Isaac and laid him on the altar, on top of the wood. ¹⁰Then he reached out his hand and took the knife to slay his son. ¹¹But the angel of the Lord called out to him from heaven, 'Abraham! Abraham!'

'Here I am,' he replied.

¹²'Do not lay a hand on the boy,' he said. 'Do not do anything to him. Now I know that you fear God, because you have not withheld from me your son, your only son.'

¹³Abraham looked up and there in a thicket he saw a ram caught by its horns. He went over and took the

B

△ Read the story from Genesis 22.1–19 and decide what is happening in this painting by Rembrandt.

ram and sacrificed it as a burnt offering instead of his son. [14]So Abraham called that place The Lord Will Provide. And to this day it is said, 'On the mountain of the Lord it will be provided.'

[15]The angel of the Lord called to Abraham from heaven a second time, [16]and said, 'I swear by myself, declares the Lord, that because you have done this and have not withheld your son, your only son, [17]I will surely bless you and make your descendants as numerous as the stars in the sky and as the sand on the seashore. Your descendants will take possession of the cities of their enemies, [18]and through your offspring all nations on earth will be blessed, because you have obeyed me.'

[19]Then Abraham returned to his servants, and they set off together for Beersheba. And Abraham stayed in Beersheba.

Genesis 22.1–19.

 Activity

This crossword contains 24 key words from the story of Abraham and Isaac but it has none of the clues. That's your job.

Make up a clue to go with each answer. An example has been done for you. Remember to include a verse where the answer can be found.

Clues

5 down *What animal did Abraham sacrifice instead of his son? Verse 13*
Or you could write it this way:
Abraham sacrificed a _____ in place of his son. Verse 13

List of clues needed

Across	Down
3	1
6	2
9	4
12	5
13	7
15	8
16	10
18	11
19	12
21	14
23	17
	20
	22
	22

The near sacrifice of Isaac

The system of sacrifices

Offering sacrifices to God formed a central part of Old Testament life, and although the sacrificial system developed mostly after Abraham died, it is a very important part of how the Jewish nation understood their relationship with God. It is how most people in the early world showed their respect to their gods.

The killing of the best of the cattle thanked God for providing pasture and food. The blood of the animals was sacred because it represented its life, which was the greatest thing they could offer. They were also supposed to give the best of their crops.

Atonement

The Israelites believed that God took an interest in them that went deeper than merely arranging good living conditions. They believed that God cared how they behaved. They soon realised that they needed a way to say sorry for the things they did wrong.

Over the years new rituals emerged – special sacrifices were offered as a way of making things right with God again. This was called ATONEMENT. This is the way most Christians understand what happened when Jesus died.

It is important to know about this way of thinking because it helps to understand why Jesus' death is seen as a sacrifice for sin. (See Unit 19.)

(See Unit 19.)

understand

Abraham's faith

God had made a covenant with Abraham that he would be the father of a great nation. God would give the people Canaan, now called Israel (Genesis 17).

Abraham's part of the covenant was to CIRCUMCISE every male in his tribe as an outward sign that they worshipped God.

The point of asking Abraham to sacrifice his son was to see whether his oath of allegiance to God really meant something to him. He had already circumcised Isaac but this was the ultimate test. The sacrifice of the first-born son was common practice at this time and although we think it is a barbaric custom today, it was very important then.

So what stopped Abraham from going through with it? He made all the preparations for the sacrifice, but he knew that his god was different from the gods worshipped by other tribes. God had promised him as many descendants as there were stars, but he had only one heir who was born in Abraham's wife's old age.

Mountain tops were thought to be nearer God, therefore appropriate places for sacrifices. Abraham heard the angel speaking to him. This may have been an external voice, or it may have been a voice he heard in his head but Abraham now realised what sacrifice was all about. The god he worshipped was far more interested in FAITH and obedience than in the primitive ritual of sacrificing children. Abraham had shown so much faith in God's promise that he would be the father of a huge nation, that he had been prepared to give up what looked like his only chance of this happening. Abraham called the mountain 'The Lord Provides' because God provided a ram in place of his son.

● ● Discuss

Why do you think God put Abraham through the misery of thinking he would lose Isaac?

● ● Think and write ...

1 Why was Abraham willing to sacrifice Isaac?
2 What do you suppose was going through Abraham's mind as he went up the mountain?
3 God blessed Abraham for having the faith to obey him in something very difficult. What was that BLESSING?

● ● Digging deeper

4 Why is this passage sometimes called the 'testing of Abraham'?
5 Why did Abraham leave the servants behind halfway through their journey?

➜ POSSIBLE APPLICATIONS

- Dietrich Bonhoeffer (page 28)
- Mother Teresa (page 138)
- Miracle on the River Kwai (page 130).

apply

understand

● ● Discuss

Abraham recognised God's voice but how might a person know today whether God was speaking to them or not?

Do people today hear God telling them to do things?

Deciding whether God is telling you to do something can be very difficult and people of all religions have experienced this over the ages. For example, Joan of Arc heard voices in her head telling her to fight the English. Was she mad or did she really hear God's voice? We'll never know. Great men of faith such as John Wesley, William Wilberforce, C.T. Studd, John Booth and Dr Barnardo all believed they heard God telling them to act in a particular way in a particular situation. They acted out of faith.

Dietrich Bonhoeffer 1906–1945

Dietrich Bonhoeffer showed tremendous faith and courage during the Second World War. He had strong Christian beliefs and was not afraid to voice them. He is an example of a man who obeyed what he believed God was telling him to do.

Dietrich Bonhoeffer was a pastor in the German Church in the 1930s. During this time Hitler was becoming more and more powerful and some of his ideas went against Christian belief. One in particular was anti-Semitism, which means being against all things Jewish. As Hitler grew in power, he began rounding up Jews everywhere and sending them to concentration camps.

The Church leaders in Germany were afraid that if they spoke out against this, they would be sent to prison too and maybe even the churches themselves would be closed. So they tried to absorb the anti-Semitic teaching into their Christian doctrine. They set up the Reich Church which agreed not to criticise Hitler. It combined Nazi beliefs with Christian beliefs. Many German Christians disagreed strongly with this; Dietrich Bonhoeffer was one of them.

In spite of being offered a place of safety in America in 1939, just before the outbreak of war, he believed God was telling him to return to Germany and preach the truth of the Christian message, and not the watered down version being offered by the State Church.

△ The logo of the Reich Church combined the Christian cross with the Nazi swastika.

▷ Nuremberg 1934: Hitler greets the evangelical Bishop Mueller and Catholic Abbot Schachleiter.

Bonhoeffer said, 'I must live through this difficult period of our national history with the Christian people of Germany. I will have no right to participate in the reconstruction of Christian life in Germany after the war if I do not share the trials of this time with my people.'

His breakaway group became known as the 'Confessing Church'. He started a secret theological college where he trained clergy.

He found out about the ultimate fate of Jews taken to camps and began helping them to escape to countries like Switzerland. He had many friends in Europe and he used these contacts to spread information about the Resistance movement in Germany. By being a member of this movement himself, he became involved in a plot to assassinate Hitler. He believed that this was the only way that Germany would be able to stop the evil of the Nazi Party.

Bonhoeffer was arrested and taken to a Gestapo prison. He spent three years in prison, mostly in solitary confinement. He was then transferred to a concentration camp at Flossenburg and executed on 9 April 1945, just months before the end of the war. The SS doctor on duty that day said that 'he was devout, brave and composed'.

●● Think and write …

1 Which particular government view worried Bonhoeffer?
2 Describe Bonhoeffer's attempts to stay true to his beliefs.

●● Digging deeper

3 In what ways was Bonhoeffer's faith tested?
4 Why did he refuse to stay in the United States in 1939?
5 Do you think he was right to become involved with an assassination attempt on Hitler?

5 Moses and the Burning Bush

● ● **Starter**
1 Have you or someone you know ever thought God might be speaking to you?
2 Have you ever seen something that you can't explain?

My Conversation with God – by Moses

I am one of those people who has not led what you might call an ordinary life. It's too long a tale to tell here but right now I am working for my father-in-law, Jethro, as a shepherd and hoping that I can live out my days peacefully. Some hope! Let me tell you what happened today and you'll see what I mean.

I was out with the sheep in the desert by the holy mountain of Horeb, which some folk call Sinai, when I saw an extraordinary thing. It was a bush and it was on fire. Fire in dry places is always a hazard but before I had time to worry about it spreading, I noticed that the branches and twigs were not actually burning up. This merited closer investigation so I went nearer to look and that is when my peaceful existence disappeared out of the window.

I heard a voice.

No, I was not imagining it. The voice said my name, 'Moses'.

So I said, 'Yes?'

And then the voice told me to take off my sandals because the ground where I was standing was holy. How scary was that? So I did of course. Then the voice said that it was God speaking. His actual words were, 'I am the God of your father, the God of Abraham, the God of Isaac and the God of Jacob'. Well, I am a Hebrew as you know, even though I was brought up as an Egyptian prince, so this was my God who was speaking to me and I'm not ashamed to tell you that I was terrified. I buried my face in my cloak because I was too afraid to look. Don't be surprised that I was afraid; I knew all the stories about our God, about how powerful he was, how he created the whole world. I knew

how he hated wrong doing and punished it, but also how he gave people every chance to reform. And yet he spoke directly to our ancestor Abraham and made a covenant with him. And now he was speaking to me!

Then we talked. I don't know if you have ever had a conversation with God, but it rather changes the way you look at things. Things you didn't see as being your business are suddenly very much your business. Jobs you thought were best done by others are suddenly jobs you find yourself agreeing to do yourself. That's what happened to me.

God said that he had seen the misery of Israelite slaves in Egypt and heard them crying out to the slave drivers. That's a dreadful sight. I know because I've seen it and heard the cries myself. Then God announced that he was so concerned about their suffering that he had decided to rescue them and lead them to safety somewhere fantastic. His actual words were, 'a land flowing with milk and

been bullying one of the slaves. If they quizzed me as to who had sent me to them what was I to say?

honey'. At the moment this land belongs to other people: the Canaanites, Hittites, Jebuzites, Amorites, Perizites and Hivites. I thought this was a good idea and the sooner God rescued them and gave them this land, the better, although I did wonder why he was telling me all this.

'So,' continued God, 'I am sending you to Pharaoh to bring my people out of Egypt.'

'Me?!' I stuttered. 'Who am I to go to Pharaoh and demand something like that?'

God said not to worry and that he'd be with me. He added we'd all come back to this spot and worship him here and that it would be a sign that he had been with us all the time. I had plenty more objections but they sounded even to my ears like lack of faith. I was a bit worried about what I would say to my own people because I had not exactly left them the best of friends. In fact, they had pretty well threatened to tell Pharaoh that I had killed one of the Egyptian task masters, which I had, because he'd

God said, '**I am who I am**'. This might sound odd to you but you have to understand that God is the founder of everything, the source of all being. He is the God of our fathers, Abraham, Isaac and Jacob. Just as he was faithful to them in the past, so he will be faithful to us in the present. This is what will convince the Israelites that God himself has sent me to them and give them the confidence to trust me.

God then told me in more detail what to say, how he would be remembered for generations and how I was to tell them that God himself promised to bring them out of Egypt into safety and plenty.

God and me, that is.

See what I mean? I had signed on the dotted line…

Read the whole story of this great leader in **Exodus 3.1–17**.

●● Think and write . . .

1 How did God attract Moses' attention?
2 What did God ask Moses to do?
3 What objections did Moses raise?
4 What was God's answer to him?
5 Why might the name 'I am who I am' influence the Hebrew slaves to follow Moses?

●● Digging deeper

6 How is this story about faith?
7 What do we learn about the character of Moses from this story?
8 These days we assume all events must have a rational explanation. Do you agree? Show that you have thought about more than one point of view.

The Burning Bush

The flame was a symbol for the presence of God. The bush was not actually burning up so the flame was fuelling itself.

It made Moses curious and attracted him to come closer where he would then hear God speak.

Fire is also a symbol for purity and holiness.

The fire revealed the glory of God.

The Revealed Character of God

God is holy – Moses was asked to take off his shoes in his presence.

God is a living active being – as opposed to the idols of pagan worship which are not alive. The name Yahweh literally means 'Being' – I am, I exist.

God is compassionate – he was moved by the suffering of his people.

God honours the covenant he made with his people. He introduced himself as the God of Abraham, Isaac and Jacob and told Moses about his intention to save his people.

understand

The Covenant Promise

Think back to God's promises to Abraham after he had been prepared to sacrifice Isaac to God. God promised to give land to his descendants. This same promise is reiterated to Moses. God describes the land as 'flowing with milk and honey'. The milk would come from sheep and goats and the honey from bees and together they would meet the needs of a nomadic nation such as the Israelites.

The land in question was populated by seven tribes but God had promised Abraham that his descendants would conquer their enemies and inhabit their land.

Moses' Call

- Moses showed a proper respect for God by removing his shoes and hiding his face.
- He was a very reluctant hero in this story. He kept coming up with reasons why he was not the best person for the job because he didn't want to go back to Egypt and face everything he had left, especially for a task that did not seem likely to be successful.
- He felt inadequate and asked what was so special about him that he should go to Pharaoh. God's answer required Moses to have faith that he would indeed bring the Israelites out of Egypt to worship on this mountain.
- He needed God's authority to lead the Israelites, which is when God revealed his name: 'I AM has sent you'. Moses had to have faith that God would be with him.

●● Think and write . . .

1 What does this story teach about the character of God?
2 What part does God's covenant with Abraham play in God's plans?
3 Make a chart to show the symbolism of the burning bush.

●● Digging deeper

4 Do you think Moses was the right man for the job God needed doing?
5 Explain why Moses was so reluctant to do it.

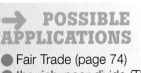

→ POSSIBLE APPLICATIONS
- Fair Trade (page 74)
- the rich–poor divide (TRB unit 11)
- the work of Oscar Romero (page 72).

Sir Trevor Huddleston and the fight against apartheid

△ Huddleston spent time working with young men, and fought for racial equality. 'If you could say that anybody single-handedly made apartheid a world issue then that person was Trevor Huddleston.' (Archbishop Desmond Tutu)

Going to Sophiatown

At university in Britain, Trevor Huddleston had been a pacifist and a Christian Socialist, believing in human equality and non-violence. He joined a tiny Anglican religious order called the Resurrection Fathers, which was committed to social action. They sent him to the African squatter township of Sophiatown (on the outskirts of Johannesburg) in 1943.

Here he came face to face with the horror and injustice of APARTHEID. Apartheid was the total separation of black and white people in South Africa. Black people had no rights and it was their housing conditions that shocked Huddleston the most. He taught black people to respect themselves by encouraging black students to take on roles of leadership within their community.

understand

apply

● ● **Discuss**

'People have to experience apartheid at first hand to be true protestors.' Do you agree?

△ Sophiatown, 1943.

Campaigning in South Africa

Huddleston became an active supporter of the African National Congress (ANC), who campaigned for equal rights for all people in South Africa. He condemned the unjust policies towards black Africans. 'If cities fall under the judgment of God ... then I have little doubt that Johannesburg will be condemned for this reason alone: that it accepted man's sweat and man's toil and denied him the possibility of a home,' he wrote.

Although Huddleston fought to save it, Sophiatown was levelled between 1955 and 1963 and its inhabitants were moved to Meadowlands in Soweto. A residential whites-only area was built in its place. It was named Triomf.

△ Marching as to war: Trevor Huddleston in Sophiatown, Johannesburg.

Writings on prejudice

- In his controversial book, *Naught for your Comfort* (published 1956), he accused South Africa of racism, prejudice and legalised persecution. The book received worldwide publicity and sparked a global debate on apartheid.
- He helped organise the committee that wrote the Freedom Charter, which sets out the main principles of the ANC, and received their highest honour, the Isitwalandwe, for his work.

Worldwide campaign

- Back in Britain he helped found Britain's Anti-Apartheid Movement in 1959 and led its campaigns for sanctions against the white-led government.
- In South Africa his nickname was 'Dauntless One' because he never gave up. He received a knighthood for his work against apartheid.
- Alan Paton, an anti-apartheid author, described Huddleston as 'one burning to serve the world', and in his film *Cry, the Beloved Country*, he modelled the priest on him.

●● Think and write ...

1 Describe how Trevor Huddleston became involved with the fight against apartheid.
2 What does the photograph of the protest march show about his fight for Sophiatown?
3 Was his anger with Johannesburg justified?
4 In what way was Trevor Huddleston's task in Africa like Moses' task in Egypt, and how was it different?

●● Digging deeper

5 What do Desmond Tutu's and Alan Paton's comments tell us about the kind of man Trevor Huddleston was?
6 How might his Christian beliefs have influenced the stand he took in South Africa?

6 Exodus and the Passover

encounter

●● **Starter**

1 Do you think people usually get what they deserve for doing wrong?

2 Do you think that corrupt governments should be brought down using force?

¹The Lord said to Moses and Aaron in Egypt, ²"This month is to be for you the first month, the first month of your year. ³Tell the whole community of Israel that on the tenth day of this month each man is to take a lamb for his family, one for each household. ⁴If any

household is too small for a whole lamb, they must share one with their nearest neighbour, having taken into account the number of people there are. You are to determine the amount of lamb needed in accordance with what each person will eat. ⁵The animals you choose must be year-old males without defect, and you may take them from the sheep or the goats. ⁶Take care of them until the fourteenth day of the month, when all the people of the community of Israel must slaughter them at twilight. ⁷Then they are to take some of the blood and put it on the sides and tops of the door-frames of the houses where they eat the lambs. ⁸That same night they are to eat the meat roasted over the

fire, along with bitter herbs, and bread made without yeast. ⁹Do not eat the meat raw or cooked in water, but roast it over the fire – head, legs and inner parts. ¹⁰Do not leave any of it till morning; if some is left till morning, you must burn it. ¹¹This is how you are to eat

it: with your cloak tucked into your belt, your sandals on your feet and your staff in your hand. Eat it in haste; it is the Lord's Passover.

¹²'On that same night I will pass through Egypt and strike down every firstborn – both men and animals – and I will bring judgement on all the gods of Egypt. I am the Lord. ¹³The blood will be a sign for you on the houses where you are; and when I see the blood, I will pass over you. No destructive plague will touch you when I strike Egypt.'

Exodus 12.1–13

Think and write . . .

1 Describe the preparations each family must make for the Passover.
2 Imagine you are a member of one such family. Write an account of the evening of the Passover.
3 What would happen on the night of the Passover?

Digging deeper

4 Explain why the event is called 'the Passover'.
5 Why must the bread be unleavened and any uneaten lamb burnt?
6 Do you think the Israelites did the right thing in running away from Egypt?
7 What kind of things might make you or your family leave your country for good?

The Passover

Jews all over the world celebrate the Passover every year and remember how God rescued them from slavery in Egypt. They re-enact the meal and tell each other the story of the Passover through the symbols of what they eat. So what must the original Passover have been like? It would certainly not have been a time of celebration; it would have been a time of great fear, anxiety and uncertainty. The Israelites had to trust that Moses really was God's messenger and that he would lead them to safety.

The theme of covenant is developed in the story of the Passover. The Israelites were God's chosen people. He had promised Abraham that he would bless his descendants and give them the cities of their enemies. He had heard their cry for help and through Moses, set about rescuing them.

understand

The significance of the preparations for Passover

1 The **new year** was to begin in the Spring and not, as previously, in the Autumn. It was also a Spring Festival of new life.

2 A **year old, male lamb without defect** was to be selected. This wasn't any old sheep; this was a valuable male which did not have anything wrong with it and would, if left, have sired healthy offspring. Only the best would do. There is a connection here for Christians between the sacrifice of the Passover lamb and the sacrifice of Jesus. Jesus is often referred to as the 'Passover Lamb'. In Christian tradition Jesus died to save people from the slavery of sin and death, just as God saved the Israelites from slavery and death at the hands of the Egyptians.

3 Some of the **blood from the lamb had to be smeared on the lintels and door posts of the house**. Blood, as we have seen before, is a symbol for life and played an important part in sacrifices. It is blood that reminds people of God's **covenant** with them. The death of the lamb by the shedding of its blood can be seen as the substitution for the death of the Israelites. When God passed through the land of Egypt, he would see the blood and pass over. The Israelites would escape the judgement of God on Egypt because of the blood. In Christian tradition the blood of Jesus does the same thing – it saves all people from the judgement of God.

4 The lamb was to be **roasted over a fire**. This was the method used by shepherds in the desert. The roasting by fire, the eating of the lamb whole and the burning of any leftovers showed the Israelites' commitment to escape and their faith in God. This was a holy event.

5 They were to eat the lamb with **bitter herbs**. Later the bitter herbs would remind them of their misery as slaves. On this night, they were a symbol of freedom.

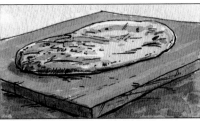

6 The **bread was to be unleavened**. This means bread made without yeast. The suddenness of the escape meant there was no time for bread to rise before baking. Also, if they were to travel, the bread would keep much longer without yeast in it.

7 The people must eat their meal **ready to travel**. This meal would not be a relaxed affair; it would be eaten quickly as they waited anxiously for God's anger to fall upon Egypt and the time for their escape.

●● Think and write ...

1 Explain the importance of the blood on the doorposts and lintel.
2 What was special about the lamb?
3 Why did they have to burn any left over bits of the roast lamb?

●● Digging deeper

4 How is God's action in this story a sign of his covenant with his people?
5 What is the link between the Passover and the death of Jesus for Christians?
6 Why do you think the Jews continue to celebrate the Passover every year?

●●● Activity

7 Make a chart to show the preparations the Israelites had to make for the Passover and the significance of each.

→ POSSIBLE APPLICATIONS

● human rights (TRB unit 7)
● Trevor Huddleston (page 34)
● men and women of faith (TRB unit 4)
● Martin Luther King (page 40)
● celebrating Passover today (TRB unit 6).

Martin Luther King: US civil rights leader

'I have a dream that one day this nation will rise up and live out the true meaning of its creed. We hold these truths to be self-evident that all men are created equal. I have a dream that my four little children will one day live in a nation where they will not be judged by the colour of their skin but by the content of their character.'

▷ Martin Luther King speaking to crowds in Selona, Alabama, in 1965.

Why did Martin Luther King start his campaign for equal rights for black people?

Four million Africans had been shipped over to America during the eighteenth and nineteenth centuries to work as slaves. Although slavery was abolished as long ago as 1869, in the mid-twentieth century many people still looked down on black people and thought they were inferior to white people.

Growing up in the southern states of America in the 1940s, King became aware that black people and white people were treated differently:

● Black people earned half what white people would earn doing the same job.
● Although in theory black people could vote, all sorts of intimidation and bureaucratic tricks were used to stop them registering their votes.

● Black children had to go to special schools and were not allowed to take the same exams as white people.
● Black people were banned from shopping in white people's shops and from sitting on white people's benches. They were allocated seats at the backs of buses.

Martin Luther King experienced this discrimination from an early age. One day, he went to a shop with his father to buy shoes. The shopkeeper refused to serve them because they were sitting on seats reserved for white people. King never forgot how he felt on that occasion and he decided to work for equal rights for all Americans, whatever the colour of their skin.

apply

How did Martin Luther King campaign?

He was a pastor in the Baptist church in the city of Montgomery, Alabama. As a Christian, he believed in non-violent protest. 'Meet hate with love,' he said.

● In 1955 he organised a **bus boycott**. The boycott meant that black people would stop using the buses until they were treated equally. The next year, a law was passed making it illegal to separate black and white people on buses.
● In the 1960s he led **demonstrations** against unfair laws in housing, hotels and restaurants.
● In 1963 he organised a **march** of hundreds of schoolchildren in Birmingham, Alabama, to protest about inferior education. They were singing and chanting and waving home-made banners. The police were sent in with dogs and high-pressure water hoses. They attacked the children, many of whom were badly injured. Pictures of these attacks were broadcast worldwide.
● In 1964 King was awarded the Nobel Peace Prize.
● In 1965 he led a **peaceful march** campaigning for voting rights for blacks. This was broken up by police using tear gas and batons. Again, pictures of the violence were broadcast to the world. The same year, the law was changed to allow equal voting opportunities for blacks.

△ Police attack children on a civil rights march, 1963.

Who opposed Martin Luther King?

● The Ku Klux Klan was a secret society of white men who hated black people.
● Malcolm X was a black Muslim who argued that violence was justified in order to end the injustice and prejudice against blacks.
● Ordinary white Americans opposed King because they had grown up with the system and never gave it much thought. As his campaign went on, many started to support him.
● Threats were made against him and his family. He was stabbed, his home was bombed, but he carried on campaigning.
● In 1968 Martin Luther King was assassinated by a white man called James Earl Ray. King's words spoken on an earlier occasion would prove true: 'When I die, my work will only just be beginning'.

●● Think and write ...

1 How were black Americans treated differently from white Americans in the 1940s and 1950s?
2 How did Martin Luther King win equal rights for blacks travelling on buses?
3 Make a list of King's achievements.
4 Who opposed King and why?
5 Imagine you were present at the Birmingham, Alabama, demonstration against inferior education in 1963. Write a letter to a friend or relative describing what you saw.

●● Digging deeper

6 Martin Luther King's work brought danger to his family. Was he right to continue with his campaign even after they had received death threats?
7 Does King's motto 'meet hate with love' work?
8 People will always make slaves of one another. Do you agree?
9 What links can you see between the story of the Passover and MLK's campaign?

7 Moses and the Ten Commandments

● ● Starter

Think about your school rules. Is there one rule that you think is essential to the smooth running of the school? And is there one you think the school could do without?

A special covenant

God had chosen the Israelites to be in a special relationship with him. He made an agreement or 'covenant' with them through Moses: God would protect and lead his people, while they would keep God's law. This covenant relationship is one of the most important themes of the Bible and is central to our understanding of both Old and New Testaments. The word 'testament' means 'covenant'.

A [1]In the third month after the Israelites left Egypt – on the very day – they came to the Desert of Sinai. [2]After they set out from Rephidim, they entered the Desert of Sinai, and Israel camped there in the desert in front of the mountain.

[3]Then Moses went up to God, and the Lord called to him from the mountain and said, 'This is what you are to say to the house of Jacob and what you are to tell the people of Israel: [4]"You yourselves have seen what I did to Egypt, and how I carried you on eagles' wings and brought you to myself. [5]Now if you obey me fully and keep my covenant, then out of all nations you will be my treasured possession. Although the whole earth is mine, [6]you will be for me a kingdom of priests and a holy nation." These are the words you are to speak to the Israelites.'

[7]So Moses went back and summoned the elders of the people and set before them all the words the Lord had commanded him to speak. [8]The people all responded together, 'We will do everything the Lord has said.' So Moses brought their answer back to the Lord.

Exodus 19.1–8.

I YOU SHALL HAVE NO OTHER GODS BEFORE ME.

II YOU SHALL NOT BOW DOWN TO OR WORSHIP ANY IMAGE.

III YOU SHALL NOT MISUSE THE NAME OF THE LORD YOUR GOD.

IV REMEMBER THE SABBATH DAY AND KEEP IT HOLY.

V HONOUR YOUR FATHER AND MOTHER.

VI YOU SHALL NOT MURDER.

VII YOU SHALL NOT COMMIT ADULTERY.

VIII YOU SHALL NOT STEAL.

IX YOU SHALL NOT GIVE FALSE TESTIMONY AGAINST YOUR NEIGHBOUR.

X YOU SHALL NOT COVET.

Read the whole passage in **Exodus 20.1–20**.

● ● **Think and write . . .**

The commandments address three key areas of the Israelites' lives: religious, social and personal.

Divide your page into three and write down which commandments belong to which key area.

Moses and the Ten Commandments

Each section is followed by some questions. Remember to give reasons for your answers.

1 You shall have no other gods before me

This was important in a land where many tribes co-existed, each having their own gods. Israel would soon lose her identity if she allowed religious integration. The Hebrew word used for God is 'YHWH' or Yahweh.

➡ England is considered by many to be a multi-cultural country. What are the advantages and disadvantages of living among people of other faiths and cultures?

3 You shall not misuse the name of the Lord your God

or do not take the Lord's name 'in vain' as traditional texts say. In later Judaism this covered any careless or irreverent use of the name 'Yahweh'. Originally the commandment referred to swearing an oath on the Lord's name, which the person had no intention of keeping, or about something that was a lie.

➡ What do we regard today as the strongest kind of oath we can make? For example, swearing on someone's life.
➡ Why is swearing frowned upon at school?
➡ What is the difference between bad language and swearing?

2 You shall not bow down to or worship any image

This commandment included making images of their own God. Yahweh was not to be worshipped in the same way as gods of other tribes were worshipped. These gods were local and their images had to be carried around with the tribe. Yahweh was not to be confined to a place although, later, the Temple and the Ark of the Covenant containing, among other things, the tablets on which the Ten Commandments were written, came to symbolise his presence.

➡ What idols do people worship today?

4 Remember the Sabbath day and keep it holy

This is a positive commandment. It commemorates the day God rested after creating the world. Not even animals were exempt from this work ban.

➡ Is a day of rest appropriate in our modern age?
➡ Find out why the Sabbath, Saturday, came to be observed by the Christian world on a Sunday.

5 Honour your father and your mother

This is another positive commandment and one which comes with a promise – 'that you may live a long time in the land . . .'. Those who build a society in which old age has an honoured place may themselves expect honour one day. This attitude towards the older generation is reflected right through the Old Testament and is found in many other ancient cultures, especially China. A settled society where there is mutual respect will be united against common enemies and at peace with itself.

➡ Would you say that today's society in Britain honours old age? Give reasons.
➡ Do you think that parents should be respected regardless of whether they deserve it?

understand

6 You shall not murder The law distinguishes between planned and accidental or unpremeditated killings (Exodus 21.12–14). The sanctity of life is seen as God's gift. There is a distinction between the Hebrew words for killing, murder and execution, so this commandment does not forbid capital punishment. 'Blood guiltiness' was something a person carried around forever. (See Unit 3.)

➡ Can killing someone ever be right?

8 You shall not steal In a peasant society where life is hard, any theft of property may lead to death because most possessions are vital to survival. This makes it a very serious crime. There is a strong link between this and the tenth commandment.

➡ Why is stealing universally considered to be wrong?
➡ Is it OK to steal from a very rich person or organisation?
➡ Do you think it would be all right to steal to provide for your family?

7 You shall not commit adultery The law allowed polygamy (having more than one wife) but it never allowed polyandry (having more than one husband). In the days of Moses, women became the property of their husbands when they married, so for a man to 'steal' another man's wife was theft of his property. It was very important that a man knew that children born to his wives were his and not someone else's because they would bear his name and have rights within his family. This law protected family lines.

➡ Do you think being faithful to your husband or wife is old-fashioned and unnecessary?

9 You shall not give false testimony against your neighbour In a simple desert community, nearly all crimes would be punishable by death. This made false accusations the same as murdering someone. To ensure that no one else was responsible for the death of an innocent person, the witness had to carry out the execution. If he were lying, he would carry the burden of blood-guiltiness.

➡ What is a lie?

10 You shall not covet The old word 'covet' means to want something that belongs to someone else. It is a strong kind of jealousy. This is the only commandment that forbids a particular attitude of mind. The word 'house' means 'household' – in the desert people would have lived in tents, and a man's wife would have been listed as the most important of all his possessions. Ox and ass are the typical wealth of the bronze-age peasant. Envy of someone else's things often leads to hurting them.

➡ If you 'covet' something that isn't yours, what other commandments might you end up breaking?

➡ **POSSIBLE APPLICATIONS**
● law and punishment (page 46)
● law and human rights (page 48)
● a possible application of one of the commandments to the modern world.

●●● **Activity**

Think about the rules in your school. In groups, select five that you think are the most important. Say why you have chosen them.

●● **Discuss**

a) Are some types of murder worse than others? For example, is killing someone in cold blood worse than killing them in a fight?

b) Do you think the relatives of the victims should have a say in what punishment criminals should have?

●●● **Activity**

1 Copy the diagram below, then add extra panels and lines to show other arguments for and against.

2 Decide which side of the argument you agree with and explain why to a partner.

Law and punishment

Just as in the days of Moses, laws need to be enforced. If people break the law, society says they should be punished.

To **deter**. To reduce crime by making the punishment severe enough to put people off offending again. Many punishments fit the crime, for example: drunk drivers lose their driving licence.

Retribution To make offenders suffer for their crimes. This shows society that law breaking will not be tolerated.

THE AIMS OF PUNISHMENT

To **protect** society from a person's anti-social behaviour.

To **reform**. To help people understand what they did wrong and change into responsible, law-abiding citizens.

Capital punishment

Many people want to bring capital punishment (the death penalty) back. Some families of murder victims feel that the murderers get off too lightly and should lose their right to life for what they did.

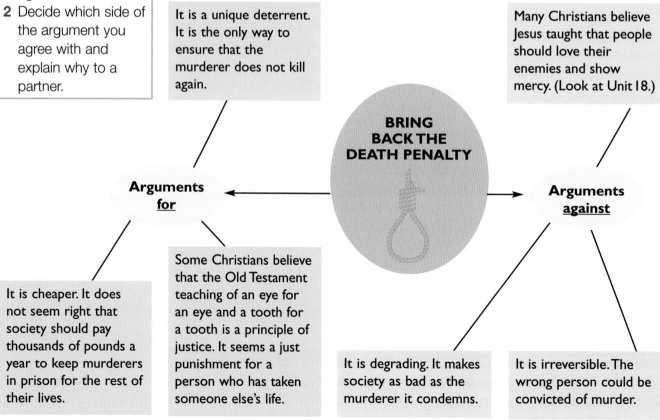

It is a unique deterrent. It is the only way to ensure that the murderer does not kill again.

Many Christians believe Jesus taught that people should love their enemies and show mercy. (Look at Unit 18.)

BRING BACK THE DEATH PENALTY

Arguments for

Arguments against

It is cheaper. It does not seem right that society should pay thousands of pounds a year to keep murderers in prison for the rest of their lives.

Some Christians believe that the Old Testament teaching of an eye for an eye and a tooth for a tooth is a principle of justice. It seems a just punishment for a person who has taken someone else's life.

It is degrading. It makes society as bad as the murderer it condemns.

It is irreversible. The wrong person could be convicted of murder.

△ Boot camps are an experiment in America at the moment. Instead of going to prison, young offenders are sent into a harsh environment. They are taught discipline, obedience and self-respect as well as practical skills. In this photo inmates at a Massachusetts camp are showing their utensils after eating.

Rehabilitation

This means helping a person to reform or change their ways. This involves education and practical support. For example, many people who turn to crime come from poor backgrounds. There is little chance of employment where they live, and they feel undervalued and ignored by society. When they get out of prison they are very likely to reoffend.

So, many employers agree to take on recently released people, and give them a chance to make a new start.

Sometimes offenders meet the victims of their crimes. The victims have been able to express their feelings and the offender has been made to listen. This has often been a healing experience on both sides.

Alternatives to prison

Sending offenders to prison does not often help them reform. Some people say it can turn petty offenders into hardened criminals because in prison they can learn from other criminals and can start taking drugs. There are a number of alternative punishments that the courts can use instead.

- Fines
- Community service
- Electronic tagging
- Anti-social behaviour orders (ASBOs)
- Loss of a licence
- Caution – the person is given a warning
- Suspended sentence – the person is given a prison sentence but does not have to serve it unless he or she breaks the law again.

●● Think and write . . .

3 Complete this chart in your book by giving at least one example of an offence which would warrant each of the above punishments.

Punishment	Offence
Fines	parking illegally
Prison	
Community service	
ASBOs	

4 Make a similar chart of the crimes and punishments in force at your school.
- Do they work?
- What would you change?
- Are the aims of punishment at your school the same as those in society? Look at the diagram on page 46.

5 Schools are no longer able to beat unruly children. This was called corporal punishment.
- **a)** Do you think schools are better places now as a result?
- **b)** Do you think *parents* should be allowed to smack their children?

●● Digging deeper

6 Do you think the boot camp method (photo A) would work in England? Give your reasons.

7 What is the purpose behind making offenders meet their victims? Do you think it is a good idea? Give your reasons.

Law and human rights

God promised to protect Israel if the people kept the Law. This type of agreement is called a covenant. There are two sides to it: rights and responsibilities. You cannot have one without the other. The idea of a covenant was to link keeping the law with being protected. The modern equivalent would be if you are law-abiding, at school or in society at large, you can expect protection and help if someone else breaks the rules and affects you.

Covenant therefore, is at the root of our law and order system: laws are based on human rights. The government protects people's human rights by laying down laws, which people obey.

Many countries today ignore this fundamental (basic) principle and operate a harsh regime which ignores people's human rights.

● ● ● Activity

1 Ask your teacher for a copy of the Declaration of Human Rights. Some of the rights relate directly to one or other of the Ten Commandments. Jot down which commandment upholds each of the rights.
2 **a)** Other rights do not seem to be addressed in any commandment. Can you think of reasons why this might be so?
   b) What laws are in place in the UK today that uphold and protect these rights?

Children's rights

The United Nations convention set out this list of rights that every child should have:

● free education
● enough food and clean water
● medical care
● time to play
● the opportunity to live with their family or those who love them
● special care if they are disabled
● a name and a nationality.

Children should be protected from:

● DISCRIMINATION
● physical, mental and sexual abuse.

Children should enjoy these rights regardless of their race, colour, religion or gender.

● ● Discuss

a) Have you ever been prevented from doing something that you thought you had a right to be doing?
b) When should it be permissible to take rights away from someone?

understand

apply 2

3 Read the following statements, which are possible rights for children. Copy this table then sort the statements into the three columns.

Important rights for children	Not very important rights for children	Children should not have these rights

I should have the right to go to bed and get up when I choose

I should have the right to wear clothes of my own choice

I should have the right to miss lessons I don't need

I should have the right to special care if I am disabled

I should have the right not to play sport

I should have the right to use a credit card

I should have the right to eat what I want when I want

I should have the right to go into town on my own

I should have the right to a healthy diet

I should have the right to watch what I like on television

I should have the right not to be physically abused in any way by an adult

I should have the right to live at home

I should have the right to be educated

I should have the right to drink alcohol

Leaders and Prophets of the Old Testament

8

David and Bathsheba; David and Nathan

key question If you have power, can you do what you like?

encounter

Read the full story in **2 Samuel 11.1–17**.

EVERYTHING EXCEPT **HER**.

SHE WAS CALLED **BATHSHEBA**.

SHE WAS BEAUTIFUL.

SHE WAS ENCHANTING.

IT WAS SPRING, THE TIME WHEN KINGS GO OFF TO WAR. I WAS LOOKING DOWN FROM THE PALACE ROOF WHEN I **SAW** HER.

OH, I HAD WIVES ENOUGH ALREADY. I HAD SONS AND DAUGHTERS, ALL THAT A MAN COULD WANT.

SHE WAS ENOUGH TO MAKE ME LOSE MY MIND WITH DESIRE.

SHE WAS ANOTHER MAN'S WIFE.

AND I DIDN'T **CARE**.

● ● Starter

Schools have their own power structure.

1 What groups of people have power in your school?
2 Have there ever been occasions when you think they have abused that power?

URIAH, HER HUSBAND WAS A **HITTITE**, ONE OF MY SPECIAL GUARD, AND AWAY FIGHTING MY WARS. UNDER LAW, SOLDIERS WERE NOT ALLOWED TO RETURN TO THEIR WIVES WHILE ON ACTIVE DUTY, AND HE WAS A MAN OF GREAT PRINCIPLE. WHILE HE SLEPT IN TENTS BENEATH THE CITY WALLS OF RABBAH I MADE LOVE TO HIS WIFE IN MY PALACE.

BATHSHEBA BECAME PREGNANT. **FOOL** THAT I WAS, I COVERED ONE EVIL WITH **ANOTHER** – I SENT URIAH ON A DANGEROUS MISSION, AND GAVE ORDERS FOR HIM TO BE LEFT **STRANDED** WHERE THE FIGHTING WAS THE THICKEST.

IT WAS AS IF I'D MURDERED HIM **MYSELF**.

A ¹The Lord sent Nathan to David. When he came to him, he said, 'There were two men in a certain town, one rich and the other poor. ²The rich man had a very large number of sheep and cattle, ³but the poor man had nothing except one little ewe lamb that he had bought. He raised it, and it grew up with him and his children. It shared his food, drank from his cup and even slept in his arms. It was like a daughter to him.

⁴'Now a traveller came to the rich man, but the rich man refrained from taking one of his own sheep or cattle to prepare a meal for the traveller who had come to him. Instead, he took the ewe lamb that belonged to the poor man and prepared it for the one who had come to him.'

⁵David burned with anger against the man and said to Nathan, 'As surely as the Lord lives, the man who did this deserves to die! ⁶He must pay for that lamb four times over, because he did such a thing and had no pity.'

⁷Then Nathan said to David, 'You are the man! This is what the Lord, the God of Israel, says: "I anointed you king over Israel, and I delivered you from the hand of Saul. ⁸I gave your master's house to you, and your master's wives into your arms. I gave you the house of Israel and Judah. And if all this had been too little, I would have given you even more. ⁹Why did you despise the word of the Lord by doing what is evil in his eyes? You struck down Uriah the Hittite with the sword and took his wife to be your own. You killed him with the sword of the Ammonites."'

2 Samuel 12.1–9.

●● Think and write …

1 In the final frame of the story strip on page 50 David says, 'It was as if I'd murdered him myself'. What did he mean?

2 Read passage A. How did Nathan show David he had done wrong?

3 In verses 10–14 Nathan describes David's punishment. Write down what you think it will be, then see if you are right.

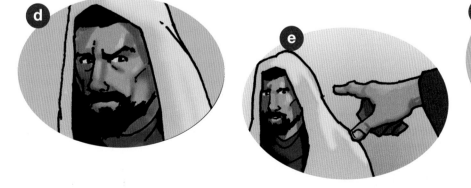

David and Bathsheba

Commentary on the text

The role of a king in those days was very specific: to protect his people from their enemies and to be a military leader. The story of David and Bathsheba shows what happens when a leader forgets his role and puts himself first. He thought that being king meant that he could do things ordinary people were not allowed to do; in this case, taking another man's wife.

When that plan failed, David arranged for Uriah to be sent on a suicide mission to attack a heavily defended stretch of town wall. David even told Joab, his commander in chief, to pull the rest of the soldiers away so that Uriah had no back up. David, who normally cared greatly for each of his soldiers, had suspended rational thought in his desire to avoid the consequences of his actions. Uriah is revealed again as a courageous and conscientious soldier.

Getting her pregnant was bad enough, but what David did next was even worse. First he sent for Uriah and tried to persuade him, even by getting him drunk, to take a break from fighting and go home, then Uriah would think the child was his. Uriah took his duties as a soldier very seriously, not giving in to temptation to leave his post even when the king himself suggested it.

However, David was prepared to marry Bathsheba. Although she lost this baby shortly after it was born, she went on to have many children, one of whom was Solomon.

▽ King David's palace, Jerusalem. It was rebuilt by Herod around the 1st century AD.

A

Nathan's parable 2 Samuel 12.1–14

Nathan was a prophet. Prophets were not always popular as their messages from God were seldom to people's liking. However, they were greatly respected and acted as advisers to leaders and kings. This enabled Nathan to tell David about God's anger.

David had allowed his physical desire to rule his head. When he heard Nathan's parable, he properly condemned the man in the story for his actions. He even spoke of the death penalty although the punishment was a fine of four times the lamb's value.

He must have been shocked when Nathan said at the end, 'You are that man' but he realised then that what he had done was unacceptable. David showed great remorse as he saw that he had not just hurt the people under his protection, but he had sinned against God. Nathan pointed out to David that God had given him everything he could want: deliverance from Saul; Saul's kingdom; and all his wives. Yet David wanted more and used his position as king to get it.

Nathan told David what the consequences would be. It is an old idea that punishment for evil deeds goes on to the next generation. It is important to distinguish between punishment and consequences. Jesus taught that a person's suffering was not the result of something their parents had done wrong. However, all actions, good and bad, have consequences and these can last for several generations. Children are greatly influenced by the way their parents behave and by the views they hold. David's family was a violent one. His own son Absolom took up arms against him and was killed, to David's terrible grief (2 Samuel 18.14–15).

●● Think and write . . .

1 Describe how David disposed of Uriah.
2 What kind of soldier was Uriah? Support your answer with evidence from the text.
3 What was David's reaction when Nathan told the story of the pet lamb?
4 What do we learn about Nathan?

Evidence   When you are asked to provide evidence for something, it means find an example that proves what you say is true.

●● Digging deeper

5 What do you think David learnt about his own actions when he realised Nathan was talking about him?
6 Nathan prophesies that some of David's descendants will die violent deaths. Is there a difference between punishment for and consequences of a wrong action? Give reasons to support your answer.
7 Does committing adultery involve breaking more than one commandment? Give reasons.

→ **POSSIBLE APPLICATIONS**
● people abusing power (page 54)
● marriage vows (TRB unit 8)
● giving in to temptation (page 90)
● leadership (page 60).

People abusing power

King David was not the first to abuse his position and he certainly wasn't the last.

Family GP **Harold Shipman** was jailed for life in January 2000 for murdering fifteen patients while pretending to help them.

At his surgery on Market Street in Hyde, patients spoke of their shock. One said, 'I couldn't fault him, he was the best doctor I have ever been to. I was heartbroken when this happened. He was very well respected here and the people loved him. This is very hard to come to terms with.'

Finlay Scott, chief executive of the GMC (General Medical Council) said, 'Doctors in this country provide high quality care and do so kindly and conscientiously. Something has gone badly wrong here. It is bound to damage public confidence, and we will have to work hard to restore that.'

Robert Maxwell took over £400m from his companies' pension funds, leaving 32,000 pensioners fearing for their future financial security.

In October 1990, an investigative journalist started looking into how Maxwell was manipulating the pension schemes of his own companies to his advantage. Maxwell died while cruising off the Canary Islands in 1991 and was found floating in the ocean. No one knows whether it was an accident, suicide or murder. The full extent of the way he misused his position only came out after his death.

understand

apply

●● Discuss

Are there any situations when it is all right to use your position to get something you want?

Jeffrey Archer appeared at the Old Bailey in 2001, facing seven charges of perverting the course of justice, perjury and dishonesty. Two charges were dropped during the trial.

Archer was an MP and deputy leader of the Conservative Party. He had an affair with a prostitute but when the story came out in the *Daily Star* in 1986, he denied it and even sued the paper for libel, which is printing something damaging about someone that is not true.

He told his secretary to alter entries in his diary and got a friend to write a letter saying he had had dinner with him at the time he was with the woman. Under oath, during the libel hearing, he swore he had not slept with the woman. He won £500,000 in damages from the paper.

Twelve years later the friend told the truth about the letter, and the paper demanded its money back. Archer was found guilty on two counts of perjury – lying under oath – and on two counts of perverting the course of justice. He was sent to prison in 2001.

British soldiers were convicted of abusing prisoners of war in Iraq in 2004. Three soldiers were thrown out of the army for this. They were disgraced and condemned by their Commanding Officers and an apology was made to the Iraqi government for the way the soldiers had misused their position.

●● Think and write . . .

1 How did each of these people abuse their position?
2 Which people do you think show the worst abuse of power? You could choose one of the examples above or think of an example of your own. Give your reasons.

●● Digging deeper

3 Power goes hand in hand with responsibility. Do you agree? Give your reasons.

encounter

● ● **Starter**

Discuss:

1 Have you ever had a dream that taught you something?

2 What would you ask for if God said you could have anything you wanted?

3 If you were the Prime Minister, what would you ask for?

WEALTH?

POWER?

WISDOM?

A ¹Solomon made an alliance with Pharaoh king of Egypt and married his daughter. He brought her to the City of David until he finished building his palace and the temple of the Lord, and the wall around Jerusalem. ²The people, however, were still sacrificing at the high places, because a temple had not yet been built for the Name of the Lord. ³Solomon showed his love for the Lord by walking according to the statutes of his father David, except that he offered sacrifices and burned incense on the high places.

⁴The king went to Gibeon to offer sacrifices, for that was the most important high place, and Solomon offered a thousand burnt offerings on that altar. ⁵At Gibeon the Lord appeared to Solomon during the night in a dream and God said, 'Ask for whatever you want me to give you.'

⁶Solomon answered, 'You have shown great kindness to your servant, my father David, because he was faithful to you and righteous and upright in heart. You have continued this great kindness to him and have given him a son to sit on his throne this very day.

⁷'Now, O Lord my God, you have made your servant king in place of my father David. But I am only a little child and do not know how to carry out my duties. ⁸Your servant is here among the people you have chosen, a great people, too numerous to count or number. ⁹So give your servant a discerning heart to govern your people and to distinguish between right and wrong. For who is able to govern this great people of yours?'

¹⁰The Lord was pleased that Solomon had asked for this. ¹¹So God said to him, 'Since you have asked for this and not for long life or wealth for yourself, nor have asked for the death of your enemies but for discernment in administering justice, ¹²I will do what you have asked. I will give you a wise and discerning heart, so that there will never have been anyone like you, nor will there ever be. ¹³Moreover, I will give you what you have not asked for – both riches and honour – so that in your lifetime you will have no equal among kings. ¹⁴And if you walk in my ways and obey my statutes and commands as David your father did, I will give you a long life.' ¹⁵Then Solomon awoke – and he realised it had been a dream.

He returned to Jerusalem, stood before the ark of the Lord's covenant and sacrificed burnt offerings and fellowship offerings. Then he gave a feast for all his court.

1 Kings 3.1–15.

● ● ● **Activity**

Choose someone you look up to and write down what it is about that person that you admire.

Read the full story in **1 Kings 3.16–28**.

Solomon's wisdom

King Solomon was the son of David and Bathsheba. People remember him for three main things:

- his great wealth
- his wisdom
- the Temple he built in Jerusalem.

This story is about Solomon's reputation for being the wisest king. It all began in a dream.

What was Solomon like as a king at this point?

- A politician – he made an alliance with his strong neighbour Egypt by marrying the King of Egypt's daughter (verse 1).
- A religious man – he worshipped God and offered sacrifices to him on the high ALTARS (verse 3). The high altars were the old altars for sacrifice in Canaan, before the Israelites moved into the land they now occupied. The high PRIEST at this time was Zadok. Once a Temple had been built, all sacrifices would be in the Temple.
- An ambitious man – he wanted to be able to rule his country with justice (verse 9).
- A humble man – he knew he was not particularly wise or experienced, as he was still a young man, probably in his late teens or early twenties (verse 7).

Solomon's dream (verses 5–14)

He had the dream the night after he had been to Gibeon to make a burnt offering. A burnt offering is when an animal is killed and then burnt whole on the altar. Burnt offerings symbolised a person's reverence and total dedication to God. He is described as UPRIGHT.

Dreams were accepted as a way God spoke to his people and as such were important.

In Solomon's dream God asks him what he would like God to give him and Solomon makes a long speech about:

- how he is honoured to have been made king after David. He was the first of the hereditary kings (verse 6).
- the many problems he has in ruling God's people (verses 8–9).
- his desire for discernment, that is, being able to know the difference between a good decision and a bad one, or good and evil as he describes it in verse 9.

God's reaction must have been a pleasant surprise for Solomon:

- God was pleased with him (verse 10).
- He would be the wisest king who had ever lived (verse 12).
- If he obeyed God's law, he would live for a long time (verse 14).

Look at what Solomon did as soon as he woke up. He went to Jerusalem and stood in front of the Covenant Box. This was a sacred box containing, among other things, the tablets of stone on which the Ten Commandments were written.

He made two kinds of sacrifice. The first was the burnt offering and the second was a fellowship offering. A fellowship offering showed a desire to stay in a right relationship with God.

After that, he did what anyone who had just been given the things he most wanted would do: he threw a party for all his officials (verse 15).

●● Think and write . . .

1 What do we learn about Solomon from what he did the day he had his dream?
2 What was the situation Solomon told God about in his dream?
3 What did Solomon ask God for specifically?
4 What do you think God expected him to reply?
5 What did God promise Solomon?

---

understand

Solomon judges a difficult case (verses 16–28)

△ *Solomon's judgement* by He Qi.

The second story is about a particular situation in which Solomon had to make a judgement, using his newly acquired wisdom. The wisdom he needed was very practical but God-given nonetheless.

It was part of a king's duties to hold a court and try cases that were too difficult for local officials. In this case there were two women, both of whom were prostitutes and very low on the social scale. This did not prevent them from receiving proper justice.

The problem
● They had both recently had babies who, as was usual, slept in the same beds as their mothers.
● One baby had been tragically crushed to death by his mother (verse 19).
● The mother had woken up and swapped the babies round while the other woman slept (verse 20).
● The other woman knew it was her baby who was alive but she couldn't prove it.

Solomon's **solution** shows an understanding of human nature. He tested their sincerity by putting the child's life in danger. The true mother was prepared to let the other woman bring up her son because at least she would be able to see him grow up.

B

Wisdom belongs to God, who made the universe and life on Earth, and it stems from having a right relationship with him.

Its origin is in the heart, which is the centre of moral and intellectual decision.

Wisdom based on knowing God's ways.

Religious wisdom means obeying God's law.

WISDOM

It means possessing technical skill.

It is understanding a situation properly.

It is formulating a workable plan to bring about the results you want from a situation.

It is the ability to judge impartially, that is, without favouring one person over another for personal reasons.

●● Think and write . . .

6 Look at diagram B. What qualities of wisdom did Solomon show when he tried the case of the two women fighting over the baby?
7 The qualities fall into three main categories. Under the headings 'spiritual wisdom', 'intellectual wisdom' and 'practical wisdom', list the qualities that fall into those categories.

→ **POSSIBLE APPLICATIONS**
● leadership (page 60).

Discuss:
1 Who are the leaders in your school?
2 Is there a difference between a leader and someone you look up to?

Leadership

What is a leader?

● A leader is someone who makes decisions on behalf of other people.
● A leader is someone to whom people go when they want the opinion of the best-qualified person in a particular field.

A

B

C

D

E

F

Who are our national leaders in Britain?

1 The **monarch** is the **Head of State** (this is currently Elizabeth II). Unlike Solomon, she does not have a big say in how the country is run but takes an active interest in politics and sometimes makes her views known. The monarch represents Britain all round the world and is respected by everyone she meets. She opens Parliament at the beginning of every new parliamentary year.

3 The **Archbishop of Canterbury** is the head of the Anglican Church throughout the world and is appointed by the Queen. His job is like that of a managing director of a company supervising other people's work but he also gives guidance about moral issues. He challenges society about its values and attitudes such as selfishness and disregard for the needs of the poor. He is ultimately responsible for how effective churches are in their communities.

2 The **Prime Minister** is the Head of Government. With advisers, he or she decides how to run the country. In the House of Commons, members of parliament hear new proposals, discuss their good points and bad points, and finally vote on whether they should become law. They make laws about all sorts of things from whether fox hunting should be banned to how much tax people should pay. They have to be ready to deal with situations that come up during their time in power. They have to manage situations such as strikes, financial crises in banks, or destructive floods like those in 2007. They often have to make important decisions with other world leaders, such as how to fight terrorism.

Who are our local leaders?

4 The **mayor** is in charge of local politics and how a town is organised. He or she is advised by locally elected men and women on issues such as traffic-calming schemes and whether schools should be closed.

6 The **headteachers** of schools make decisions about how children are taught in their schools. They are responsible for the academic standards and behaviour of the pupils. They make and enforce the school rules. They are also responsible for the health and well-being of their pupils. They influence how children think about moral issues and give them guidance and opportunities for exploring the kind of people they want to be.

5 The **vicar** of a church is a spiritual leader in the local community and people go to him or her for advice or for comments on issues. He or she has authority to baptise, marry and bury people.

●● Think and write . . .

1 Look at photos A–F.
  a) Match them to the descriptions of leaders 1–6.
  b) Have any of leaders 1–3 changed since this book was published?
2 What qualities should the following leaders have?
  a) prime minister   **b)** headteacher   **c)** vicar.

●● Digging deeper

3 How does experience help you to make better decisions as you get older?
4 Can a bad person be a good leader? Give your reasons.

10 Elijah and the prophets of Baal

key question: What happens when we stand up for what we believe?

encounter

1 Do you think it's more important to get on with people and be liked, or to stand up for what you think is right? Can you think of a time when these priorities have been in conflict for you?

2 Look at this line. Discuss where you would put yourself for a given situation.

Give in to make others happy ⟵⟶ Stand up for your principles whatever the cost

understand

BAAL CHALLENGED!

Read 1 Kings 18.20–29
Discuss: How did Baal fail his priests?

CHAOS ON CARMEL

AND GOD ANSWERED.

Read 1 Kings 18.30–39
Discuss: How did Elijah prove to the people that Yahweh was the true God?

³⁰Then Elijah said to all the people, 'Come here to me.' They came to him, and he repaired the altar of the Lord, which was in ruins. ³¹Elijah took twelve stones, one for each of the tribes descended from Jacob, to whom the word of the Lord had come, saying, 'Your name shall be Israel.' ³²With the stones he built an altar in the name of the Lord, and he dug a trench round it large enough to hold two seahs of seed. ³³He arranged the wood, cut the bull into pieces and laid it on the wood. Then he said to them, 'Fill four large jars with water and pour it on the offering and on the wood.'

³⁴'Do it again,' he said, and they did it again.

'Do it a third time,' he ordered, and they did it the third time. ³⁵The water ran down around the altar and even filled the trench.

³⁶At the time of the sacrifice, the prophet Elijah stepped forward and prayed: 'O Lord, God of Abraham, Isaac and Israel, let it be known today that you are God in Israel and that I am your servant and have done all these things at your command. ³⁷Answer me, O Lord, answer me, so these people will know that you, O Lord, are God, and that you are turning their hearts back again.'

³⁸Then the fire of the Lord fell and burned up the sacrifice, the wood, the stones and the soil, and also licked up the water in the trench.

³⁹When all the people saw this, they fell prostrate and cried, 'The Lord – he is God! The Lord – he is God!'

1 Kings 18.30–39.

450 PRIESTS OF BAAL DIE IN MASS SLAUGHTER

Read 1 Kings 18.40
Discuss: Why did the people want to kill the prophets of BAAL?

DRENCHED!

Read 1 Kings 18.41–46
Discuss: How did the weather change?

ENCOUNTER WITH GOD

Read 1 Kings 19.11–18
Discuss: What was Elijah's experience on the mountain?

PROPHET FLEES

IT HADN'T RAINED FOR **YEARS**, AND NOW THE HEAVENS OPENED. IT POURED AND POURED.

TAKING ADVANTAGE OF THE CONFUSION, ELIJAH FLED FOR HIS LIFE...

Read 1 Kings 19.1–10
Discuss: What were Elijah's thoughts as he ran away and hid in the cave?

●●● Activity

You work for a local newspaper. Write an article under one of the headings on this page or make up one of your own. You may put in more 'photographs'. You could do this on the computer.

Elijah and the prophets of Baal

Elijah was one of the greatest Old Testament prophets. His role was to be political and spiritual adviser to the kings of Israel.

Ahab was the king of Israel, the Northern Kingdom. He was a weak man, who allowed Baal worship in his kingdom.

Jezebel was married to Ahab. She brought Baal worship to Israel.

Background

The drought had already lasted for three and a half years and showed no signs of ending. There would probably have been sacrifices going on in the countryside in the hopes that Baal would send rain for the crops. Baal was a Canaanite god and the Israelites had a history of turning away from Yahweh to worship Baal. According to the Old Testament, this idolatry was Israel's most serious sin, and that is why Elijah took such drastic action to show Baal up to be a false god.

The people were worried about the drought and were not sure whether to pray to Baal or Yahweh, so Elijah challenged Ahab to a duel and arranged a contest between Israel's god Yahweh and Baal. Whichever god sent fire to ignite a special sacrificial offering was the true god. This would decide the matter once and for all. Everyone was invited to watch. The faith of the nation was at stake, which makes this one of the most significant events in the Bible.

The contest on Mount Carmel (1 Kings 18.19–46)

▽ A stone carving of Baal.

A

1 The prophets of Baal had first go and danced around the altar for hours while Elijah taunted them. They even cut themselves as a symbol of their own self-sacrifice and to show they were earnest. It was all to no avail. Nothing happened.

2 Elijah wanted the Israelites to be in no doubt of God's power so his preparations were an important part of the whole display. He rebuilt the old altar, using twelve stones. These stones symbolised the twelve tribes of Israel and so demonstrated that God was the god of both the kingdoms – the ten tribes who lived in Israel, and the two tribes that were in Judah. Note too that he poured twelve jars of water over the sacrifice.

3 Elijah's PRAYER to God was very simple in contrast to the way the prophets of Baal prayed and God answered immediately.

Various theories have been put forward to explain how the sacrifice spontaneously combusted and these are interesting but the point is not the 'how' but the fact that this MIRACLE happened when it did, convincing the people of God's power and authority.

4 What happened next seems, on the surface, to be unnecessarily brutal and violent. By killing the 450 prophets of Baal, Elijah ensured that as time went by, no one would be able to spread the rumour that it had been Baal who had lit the sacrifice and not God.

5 The last part of the chapter is about the arrival of the rain. The people of Israel had seen for themselves the power of God and turned back to him. At this point the rain, for which they had been waiting for three years, came. Elijah ran ahead of Ahab's chariot all the way back to Jezreel, some seventeen miles (over 27km). This was the act of a loyal servant of the crown, and showed Ahab that Elijah was still his true servant.

The still small voice (1 Kings 19.1–18)

● Jezebel threatened Elijah so he left Israel and went to Sinai, where he lived in a cave.
● He was very depressed about what he saw as his failure and Israel's disobedience of the law of God. He could also have been angry with God for not protecting him from Jezebel.
● God spoke to Elijah in a way that commanded his attention because it was so different from the way he expected God to speak. He expected God to answer him in a dramatic way but when he heard the soft whisper, he recognised God's presence in the stillness and realised God was speaking in his heart.
● God told him to continue to carry out his duties as his prophet and to appoint a successor.

● ● Discuss

1 Was it necessary to kill the prophets of Baal?

● ● Think and write …

2 Who was Baal?
3 Why was worshipping Baal a serious sin for Israel?
4 Was Elijah right to stand up to Ahab? Give reasons for your answer.

● ● Digging deeper

5 Why was it significant that Elijah built his altar using twelve stones?
6 Explain the connection between the contest on Mount Carmel and the coming of the rain.

● ● Discuss

7 Talk about an example of when you had a particularly wonderful time and then felt rather flat and depressed afterwards.

● ● Think and write …

8 Imagine you were Elijah sitting in the cave listening out for God. Describe what happened and what you thought.
9 Explain what Elijah learnt about God through this experience.

→ POSSIBLE APPLICATIONS

● celebrity (page 66)
● men and women of courage, for example, Martin Luther King (page 40), Oscar Romero (page 72) and Trevor Huddleston (page 34).

Why are we fascinated by celebrities?

▷ David and Victoria Beckham.

Other gods drew the Israelites towards them in Old Testament days. Today it is celebrities who fascinate us because they appear to occupy a world where dreams come true. They are rich and glamorous, glitzy and famous, and they present an image of ourselves as we wish we could be.

● ● Discuss

a) What makes someone a celebrity?
b) Who is your favourite celebrity and why?

understand

apply

In the past, celebrities were people who had achieved something such as a new invention; today people become celebrities for doing very little. Actors in television soaps become celebrities; sportsmen and women and rock stars alike are idolised. They give us, the public, what we want, which is a chance to dream about inhabiting a different world, far away from our humdrum existence. We dream about being rich and having everything we could wish for, about being successful and popular. However, we also know deep down that it is only a dream, and that the celebrity lifestyle is not real and cannot bring lasting happiness or contentment.

If we worship a celebrity, we are celebrating what that person stands for, but underneath the glamour, they are only human beings like us. When a celebrity is caught out for some misdemeanour, we are shocked, just as the Israelites were shocked to find Baal could not deliver the fire.

△ Photographers known as paparazzi follow celebrities' every move.

● ● Think and write . . .

1 What do we expect of our celebrities?
2 Why do so many people need a celebrity culture?

● ● Digging deeper

3 'Celebrity figures influence the way society behaves.' Do you agree? Give your reasons.

Leaders and
Prophets
of the Old
Testament

11

Isaiah the
prophet

key question

What is social
justice?

● ● **Starter**

Do we have a duty to the poor outside our own country?

Israel's sin

A

¹⁰Hear the word of the Lord,
  you rulers of Sodom;
listen to the law of our God,
  you people of Gomorrah!
¹¹'The multitude of your sacrifices –
  what are they to me?' says the Lord.
'I have more than enough of burnt offerings,
  of rams and the fat of fattened animals;
I have no pleasure
  in the blood of bulls and lambs and goats.

¹²When you come to appear before me,
  who has asked this of you,
  this trampling of my courts?
¹³Stop bringing meaningless offerings!
  Your incense is detestable to me.
New Moons, Sabbaths and convocations –
  I cannot bear your evil assemblies.
¹⁴Your New Moon festivals and your appointed feasts
  my soul hates.
They have become a burden to me;
  I am weary of bearing them.
¹⁵When you spread out your hands in prayer,
  I will hide my eyes from you;
even if you offer many prayers,
  I will not listen.
Your hands are full of blood,

Isaiah 1.10–15.

God's remedy

B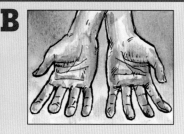

¹⁶wash and make yourselves clean.
Take your evil deeds
  out of my sight!
Stop doing wrong,
  ¹⁷learn to do right!
Seek justice,
  encourage the oppressed.

Defend the cause of the fatherless,
  plead the case of the widow.
¹⁸'Come now, let us reason together,'
  says the Lord.
'Though your sins are like scarlet,
  they shall be as white as snow;
though they are red as crimson,
  they shall be like wool.
¹⁹If you are willing and obedient,
  you will eat the best from the land;
²⁰but if you resist and rebel,
  you will be devoured by the sword.'
    For the mouth of the Lord has spoken.

Isaiah 1.16–20.

Isaiah's parable of the vineyard

C

¹I will sing for the one I love
  a song about his vineyard:
My loved one had a vineyard
  on a fertile hillside.
²He dug it up and cleared it of stones
  and planted it with the choicest vines.
He built a watchtower in it
  and cut out a winepress as well.
Then he looked for a crop of good grapes,
  but it yielded only bad fruit.
³'Now you dwellers in Jerusalem and men of Judah,
  judge between me and my vineyard.
⁴What more could have been done for my vineyard
  than I have done for it?
When I looked for good grapes,
  why did it yield only bad?

⁵Now I will tell you
  what I am going to do to my vineyard:
I will take away its hedge,
  and it will be destroyed;
I will break down its wall,
  and it will be trampled.
⁶I will make it a wasteland,
  neither pruned nor cultivated,
  and briers and thorns will grow there.
I will command the clouds
  not to rain on it.'
⁷The vineyard of the Lord Almighty
  is the house of Israel,
and the men of Judah
  are the garden of his delight.
And he looked for justice, but saw bloodshed;
  for righteousness, but heard cries of distress.

Isaiah 5.1–7.

Think and write ...

1 Look at A. What were the main reasons God was angry with the people of Israel?
2 Look at B. Make a list of God's commands to the people of Israel.
3 What does he offer in return for their obedience?
4 Look at C. Describe the vineyard God had made.
5 Why did he decide to destroy it?
6 Why does Isaiah put his message in the form of a parable about a vineyard?

Digging deeper

7 What do passages A and B tell us about the way the people of Israel were living at the time of Isaiah?
8 What kind of forgiveness did God offer in passage A?
9 In passage C, what do you think 'yielded only bad fruit' (Isaiah 5.2) means?
10 Explain how disobedient Israel is described (Isaiah 5.5–7).

understand

⬤ ⬤ **Discuss**

Is the world today like Israel and Judah at the time of Isaiah?

Background

Isaiah was a prophet who lived at the time of King Hezekiah in around 740 BC. He lived at the same time as other prophets in the Bible such as Amos and Hosea. His name has an appropriate meaning for a man with his mission in life: it means 'the Lord saves'.

Isaiah wrote at a time when the kingdoms of Israel and Judah were prosperous. As a result of controlling key trade routes, some people became very wealthy and lived in great luxury. This time of ease and wealth brought with it arrogance and a lack of concern with the poverty at the bottom end of society.

The leaders of Israel may have been worshipping God, but they were worshipping foreign gods as well.

However, this prosperity was about to end because waiting in the wings was the power-greedy Assyrian king, Tiglath-Pileser III, who was building an empire and uprooting entire populations. Anyone who resisted met a hideous end.

Isaiah realised that the only way for Israel to have a hope against Tiglath-Pileser was by repenting and returning to a life of faith in God rather than making desperate alliances with pagan countries. This is what motivated him to write and speak as he did.

The Text

Isaiah 1

God's demand for social justice goes to the heart of what was wrong with the people of Israel. They might have paid lip service to God and appeared to be holy, but they did not put the spirit of the law into practice. They offered sacrifices, organised religious festivals such as that of the New Moon, and they said their prayers, but they were hypocrites and did not live holy lives. Social justice is a recurring theme in the Old and New Testaments.

Isaiah says that God offers a way forward. He talks of 'reasoning together'. This kind of speech is the kind that happens in a court of law. God was calling his people to the bar of his justice, where they would of course be found guilty. However, God says all their sins however bad (the colours scarlet and crimson refer to the blood-stained hands of murderers), will be taken away and the people will have a fresh start (snow and wool being naturally white without any bleaching). However, this forgiveness is conditional and Isaiah draws attention to the dire consequences of continuing as they had been before.

Isaiah 5 The Song of the Vineyard

This is a parable about a God who has given everything to his people but they have rejected him.

- The vineyard is Israel and Judah. The song begins in a way that will attract listeners who want to hear a love song about God and his people. For a while they hear what they expect and want to hear, but then the mood changes and an unexpected question is asked: 'what more could I have done?' The care that went into that vineyard should have produced a good crop of grapes, but it didn't. It should have been a sobering thought that God's power, wisdom and care had exhausted itself.

- The bad crop of grapes is the people of Israel. They had been given everything – all the preparations pointed to permanence: the watchtower and the winepress cut out of rock. They wanted to rule according to their values and not listen to God. This meant worshipping idols, forgetting their responsibility to the poor and oppressed, and living lives of greedy self-indulgence. So the preparations for their future were no longer needed and would be torn down.

- The tearing down of the vineyard, described in verses 5–6, is a metaphor for the destruction of Israel in the north and Judah in the south that would come at the hands of the Assyrians.

The boundaries would no longer be protected so Israel and Judah would be open to invasion.

Thorns and brambles would grow up – alien ideas, customs and beliefs would spread out of control.

There would be no rain to give life to the soil – there would be nothing to give life to the human soul.

●● Think and write . . .

1 What sort of people was Isaiah speaking to?
2 Describe the situation in Israel at the time of Isaiah.
3 Explain what God meant by 'reasoning together'.
4 What is the meaning of the phrase 'though they [your sins] are red as crimson, they shall be like wool'?
5 Explain the meaning of the parable of the vineyard.

●● Digging deeper

6 Do you think Isaiah's parable was a good one? Give your reasons.
7 Suggest why people would have reacted in several different ways to Isaiah's parable.
8 The world does not care for the oppressed and poor any more than it did at the time of Isaiah. Do you agree? Give your reasons and show that you have considered more than one point of view.

→ **POSSIBLE APPLICATIONS**

- Oscar Romero (page 72)
- Fair Trade (page 74)
- Forgiveness (page 124)
- Trevor Huddleston (page 34)
- Martin Luther King (page 40).

Oscar Romero and the fight for justice in El Salvador

An ordinary man

Oscar Romero was born in 1917 in the town of Ciudad Barrios in the mountains of El Salvador. He started out as a carpenter but eventually trained as a priest and was ordained in Rome.

He returned home and worked as a parish priest until, at the age of 50, he was made Archbishop of San Salvador.

Social unrest

At the time there was growing unrest in the country and, like many South American states, El Salvador did not always have a politically stable government. The President ruled by using the army to enforce the law. Landowners did not pay their workers a fair wage; many workers went hungry and anyone who complained was killed or just 'disappeared'.

Most people in El Salvador are Catholic and large numbers of poor people came together to challenge the injustice on religious grounds. They believed that they could not serve God if they supported a government that ignored human rights. They formed farm co-operatives and elected pastors who would speak for them on issues of social justice. Landowners were alarmed and action was taken against the workers who were involved. People were attacked by the press and disappeared without trace. In San Salvador, peaceful protests ended in violence from the soldiers.

Discuss

a) Was Romero right to get involved with politics? Give your reasons.

b) Explain why his actions led to his death.

Romero makes a stand

Up to this point Oscar Romero had gone about his work quietly; he believed the Church should not be involved in politics. But then his first bishop and close friend Rutilio Grande was murdered because he defended what the workers were doing. Romero realised that he had to stand up for justice, however great the cost.

His superiors in the Church were horrified at the change in him as he supported the poor. The poor themselves, on the other hand, were amazed and pleased because they had never expected him to take their side.

Romero began to campaign for justice and preached sermons about society's need to change so that children did not die of starvation and disease, and people could find properly paid jobs. He challenged the rulers of El Salvador to share their wealth and stop the murders.

He refused to attend any government functions until the people were treated fairly. He kept that promise and, in doing so, won the enmity of the government but the love of the people. He was threatened.

Martyrdom

One Sunday morning in March 1980 he was taking Mass. In his sermon he compared himself to a grain of wheat that grows in the soil to produce new life. He urged soldiers to stop doing evil and not follow orders that contradicted the law of God. As he was about to bless the bread and the wine, he was shot and killed.

Earlier he had had a premonition that he would die but his faith in the resurrection strengthened him. 'I do not believe in death without resurrection,' he said. 'If they kill me, I will be resurrected in the Salvadorean people.'

1 In the 1960s El Salvador was ruled by 14 of its richest land-owning families. Law and order were maintained by violence.

2 There were extremes of wealth and poverty.

These people have nothing. Why doesn't the Church do more for them?

3 Romero believed that the situation in El Salvador was unjust. But as a leader of the Roman Catholic Church he did not believe he should get involved in politics.

4 Then a close friend of Romero who had spoken out against the government was shot by the police.

5 Romero changed his mind. By not resisting the government he felt he was helping to prolong injustice. He became leader of a powerful opposition movement.

7 On 21 March 1980 …

6 He was threatened.

8 Romero's death became a symbol uniting many Christians in their struggle to change El Salvador. A fair and democratic government was finally established in 1991.

Fair Trade

△ 'Before you've finished your breakfast this morning, you'll have relied on half the world.' (Martin Luther King)

understand

apply 2

● ● **Discuss**

What should our first priority be: to get what we need as cheaply as possible for our families, or to support an unknown worker's family by paying a fairer price for his products?

Fair Trade is a growing international movement, which makes sure that producers in poor countries get a fair deal. This means a fair price for their goods (one that covers the cost of production and guarantees a living income); long-term contracts which provide real security; and, for many, support to gain the knowledge and skills that they need to develop their businesses and increase sales. It means the difference between a hand-to-mouth existence and being able to plan for the future.

The Fair Trade movement is one of the most far-reaching solutions to the problems facing producers of food and goods in poor countries. It gives those who buy the produce in the shops an opportunity to use their purchasing power to tilt the balance, however slightly, in favour of the poor.

More retailers than ever are stocking Fair Trade goods, the number of products on offer continues to grow as demand increases, and more poor communities are feeling the benefits.

Chocolate

We eat an estimated **forty billion pounds** (£40,000,000,000) worth of chocolate every year. Over the years the price of cocoa has gone down, leaving millions of families who depend on cocoa production facing extreme poverty.

In Ghana, the Fair Trade organisation has helped set up the Kuapa Kokoo Co-operative. Its 35,000 members get a fair share of the profits because when they sell to Fair Trade partners in Europe, it gets a guaranteed minimum price, and some money called a social premium, which is invested in local community projects such as digging wells. This means that even when times are hard, Kuapa's farmers still have a secure income.

△ Colin Firth is one of a number of leading actors and musicians who support Oxfam's Make Trade Fair campaign. In April 2005 they were photographed with various food and drink being dumped on them, to highlight the injustice of global trade rules and agricultural dumping on poor countries.

Coffee

Growers of coffee can suffer as well. Without Fair Trade, farmers have to sell their coffee at market prices, however low they fall. Sometimes the price doesn't even cover their costs. This means that their children cannot go to school and their families go hungry.

Colin Firth, the actor who starred in *Bridget Jones's Diary,* supports Oxfam's coffee campaign because he thinks that consumers should know the true story behind their cups of coffee. He says, 'The coffee shop is a dominant feature of the high street; we take it for granted. But the farmers who grow the beans that make the coffee we drink live in destitution; it is the big companies which are making the profits.'

As coffee is one of Haiti's few exports, Oxfam is helping to set up co-operatives to enable the small-scale growers to sell their coffee at a decent price. The Co-operative Sainte Helene Carise for example, sells direct to the European Fair Trade market.

△ By selling Fair Trade goods, shops like the Co-op help to provide a better standard of living for farmers in developing countries.

Price per pound of coffee	FREE MARKET	FAIR TRADE
January 1989	$1.21	$1.26
October 2001	$0.45	$1.21

△ Fair Trade guarantees a minimum price for farmers.

●● Think and write ...

1 Look at picture A showing a typical breakfast.
   a) Where might the items come from?
   b) What did Martin Luther King mean by his comment?
2 What is Fair Trade?
3 How is Fair Trade helping the cocoa and coffee growers?

●● Digging deeper

4 Explain how Fair Trade helps to secure justice for the poor. Give examples.
5 'The richer your family, the more you should help the poor.' Do you agree? Give your reasons.

Introduction to the New Testament

ISRAEL
circa 4 BC

GALILEE

CAPERNAUM

MAGDALA

SEA of GALILEE

NAZARETH

GADARA

CAESAREA

SAMARIA

JERICHO

RIVER JORDAN

TEMPLE

PHARISEES

JERUSALEM

BETHANY

PEREA

BETHLEHEM

JUDEA

HEBRON

ROMAN SOLDIER

DEAD SEA

The beginning of the Gospel

- Jesus was born in about 4 BC into an ordinary working class Jewish family. He had no religious training but became a RABBI, a religious teacher. There were many teachers at that time, who each hoped their own little band of DISCIPLES would pass on their message after they had died. They were all men and some had extraordinary gifts and wisdom. Jesus followed this pattern but, unlike the others, his teaching had its greatest impact outside Israel. Within twenty years of his execution, every major centre in the Roman world had at least one group of his followers.

- Jesus' disciples faced great hardship and persecution and although, with hindsight, we know Christianity became a major world religion, for them it was not a foregone conclusion. However, because Alexander the Great had built a huge empire, the ancient world was dominated by the Greek culture, which worked to the disciples' advantage. There were few language barriers and Roman roads made communication and travel easier.

The ways people thought in the ancient world

- The **Stoics** believed that if you wanted to enjoy a good life, you must live in a moral way, listening to your conscience and your reason. They did not believe in an afterlife.

- The **Epicureans** had a completely different view. They believed that because death is the end of everything, you must make the most of this life while you can. A good life consisted of balancing pleasure and reason.

- The **Gnostics** believed that there was a spiritual afterlife where God lives, but that there was no connection between the spiritual world and life on Earth. This meant that some Gnostics thought that nothing they did in the material world had anything to do with the spiritual world so they did what they liked.

Judaism is the religion of the Jews. There were Jews living in most towns and cities in the Roman Empire and they brought their beliefs and lifestyle with them. Many Romans and Greeks joined them as 'proselytes', those who took on all the demands of the Law, and as 'God Fearers', they accepted the morality of the Old Testament. Paul the Apostle made a point of always preaching the Gospel to the Jewish community first wherever he went.

● ● Discuss

Which 'philosophy' do you find the most attractive and why?

● ● Think and write ...

1 How was Jesus like the other rabbis of his day?
2 Look at the second point about how the Gospel began. How did the situation in the ancient world help the spread of Christianity?

Who was who in Israel at the time of Jesus?

PHARISEES

- They started during the exile, when the Israelites were living in Babylon. They called themselves the Hasidim which means 'God's loyal ones'. They worked out a way in which the Israelites could keep their national identity even while not in their own country. This was by strictly observing the rules of the Torah, which is the Law given to Moses, and some extra rules.
- They were not priests but they kept themselves separate from ordinary people in case they were made ritually unclean, which would mean special washing before being able to enter the Temple.
- They were middle class and their power was in the SYNAGOGUES.
- They believed in life after death, angels and demons.
- Most SCRIBES were also Pharisees.
- They came into conflict with Jesus because of their legalistic approach to religion, that is, the way they thought that religion was only about being seen to obey every law and not about the state of their hearts.

SCRIBES

- Most of them were Pharisees.
- Their job was to copy the Law onto scrolls.
- They became experts in the Law and often advised people on it.

SADDUCEES

- They were upper-class, rich landowners.
- They were priests.
- They did not believe in life after death, angels or demons.
- Their power was in the Temple.

ZEALOTS

- They were freedom fighters.
- They sparked off the great rebellion which led to the Roman destruction of Jerusalem in AD 70
- At least one of Jesus' disciples was a Zealot: Simon.
- The extreme branch of the Zealots was called the Sicarii after the long knives they used to assassinate Romans and collaborators (Jews who worked for the Romans).

The SANHEDRIN
- This was the Supreme Court at Jerusalem.
- It was made up of 70 councillors and the High Priest.
- It had wide powers in both civil and religious matters.
- It could not pass the death sentence under Roman rule. That is why Jesus had to be sent to Pilate.

Disciples
- The word means learner or pupil.
- Jesus had twelve disciples.

Some of the titles given to Jesus

1 Rabbi
This means 'teacher'. Some were attached to synagogues; others travelled around and had their own band of disciples.

2 Messiah
This is a Hebrew word meaning Anointed One. The Messiah was God's chosen one and some thought he would be king. Jesus understood it to mean one who suffers for the people.

Jesus was first recognised as the Messiah by Peter at Caesarea Philippi (Unit 17).

3 CHRIST
This is the Greek word for Messiah. Jesus is called 'Jesus Christ' for this reason.

4 SON OF GOD
Jesus had a special relationship with God, whom he called Father. The Gospels record God's voice from HEAVEN calling Jesus 'my son' both at his BAPTISM and later at his transfiguration.

5 SON OF MAN
Jesus referred to himself as the Son of Man. By doing so, Jesus identified with human suffering. He was the perfect example of how God's will can be carried out by human beings in this world. The Son of Man would also be God's judge.

Pontius Pilate
- He was a middle-class Roman administrator.
- He was appointed Procurator of Israel in AD 26.
- He appointed the High Priest and controlled the Temple funds. One of his plans was to use this money to build an aqueduct, which was not popular with the Jews.
- He could sentence a man to death.

●●● Activity

'Who am I?'
Read these statements and work out from the information on pages 76–79, who or what is the 'I' in each one:

1 I do not believe in life after death.
2 I helped to spark off the great rebellion.
3 I am a pupil and one of the twelve.
4 I copy the Law onto scrolls.
5 I and my friends assassinate collaborators with our long knives.
6 I control the Temple funds.
7 I am a teacher and have my own followers.
8 I keep myself separate from ordinary people in case they make me unclean.
9 I belong to a group known as 'God's loyal ones'.
10 I am the Supreme Court in Jerusalem.
11 My name is Greek and means Saviour.
12 I am a priest and a landowner.
13 I was Procurator of Israel in AD 26.
14 It is my destiny to suffer and die.
15 I advise on matters to do with the Law.

Jesus' Life,
Death and
Resurrection

12

The birth
of Jesus

key question

Why do we
celebrate
Christmas?

encounter

● ● Starter

Why do we all love a baby?

A ¹⁸This is how the birth of Jesus Christ came about: His mother Mary was pledged to be married to Joseph, but before they came together, she was found to be with child through the Holy Spirit. ¹⁹Because Joseph her husband was a righteous man and did not want to expose her to public disgrace, he had in mind to divorce her quietly.

²⁰But after he had considered this, an angel of the Lord appeared to him in a dream and said, 'Joseph son of David, do not be afraid to take Mary home as your wife, because what is conceived in her is from the Holy Spirit. ²¹She will give birth to a son, and you are to give him the name Jesus, because he will save his people from their sins.

²²All this took place to fulfil what the Lord had said through the prophet: ²³'The virgin will be with child and will give birth to a son, and they will call him Immanuel' – which means, 'God with us'.

²⁴When Joseph woke up, he did what the angel of the Lord had commanded him and took Mary home as his wife. ²⁵But he had no union with her until she gave birth to a son. And he gave him the name Jesus.

Matthew 1.18–25.

The story of Jesus' birth marks the beginning of his life on Earth, a life that would last for thirty-three years and end in his crucifixion. His life, death and resurrection gave rise to the birth of the Christian faith.

● ● Think and write ...

1 What was Joseph's reaction to Mary's pregnancy?
2 What made Joseph change his mind?
3 What does the name 'Jesus' mean?
4 According to Matthew, what prophecy did this fulfil?
5 What kind of a man was Joseph?

● ● Digging deeper

6 What do the names 'Jesus' and 'Immanuel' tell us about the baby?
7 Look at the Christmas decoration. Why does it show a cross?
8 What do the crib and the cross tell us about God's plan for humanity?

● ● ● Activity

Make a word search using as many of these key words from the passage as you can. You may add other words as long as they are in the story.

JESUS	MARY	JOSEPH	SON	IMMANUEL
PROPHET	DREAM	ANGEL	SINS	SAVE
RIGHTEOUS	HOLY	SPIRIT	LORD	
VIRGIN	CONCEIVED			

● ● **Discuss**

a) What was special about Jesus?

b) What are angels?

understand

Matthew's account of Jesus' birth

God's plan

In Unit 2 the question was asked, 'Why do we read the story of the Fall at Christmas?' Ever since the first man and woman were sent out from the presence of God, God has been trying to reconcile them with himself. This is essentially the theme of the Bible and indeed of Christianity. Human beings have also been trying to find their way back to God and the Old Testament is full of such stories.

Each time, God's forgiveness and faithfulness to Israel is recorded and some of his plans for the future salvation of all people are revealed. As we discovered in Unit 4, making sacrifices was the only way to approach God. God's plan for salvation also involved a sacrifice, that of his son Jesus. This story is the beginning of the working out of that plan, a plan that would end with the sacrificial death of Jesus.

Isaiah's prophecy

Isaiah prophesied that a young girl would have a special child, born in special circumstances and given a special title. The title was Immanuel, which means 'God with us'. God chose to take part in human history as a human being in the person of Jesus. This is called the INCARNATION.

There is a lot of debate about whether Jesus' birth was a miracle because if Mary was a virgin then she couldn't have become pregnant in the usual way. Some people think that Matthew is saying that as Mary is a 'young girl' (i.e. unmarried) rather than a 'virgin', then the story is explaining how her pregnancy was not a miracle but part of God's plan. On the other hand some people think if God's purpose was to become fully one with humans then the miracle is that Mary's pregnancy was caused by God. Either way, the baby's name, Jesus (which is the Greek form of the Hebrew name 'Joshua', which means 'saviour'), symbolises God's saving act.

Jesus, the Messiah

In his gospel, Matthew often shows that Jesus is the fulfilment of Old Testament prophecies about the Messiah. In chapter 1, for example, Matthew uses Jesus' family tree to show that Jesus could trace his ancestry right back to Abraham, as all true Jews could, and also that he was descended from King David. This was important because Matthew now has strong evidence to show that Jesus is the long-awaited Messiah.

So what about Joseph?

Jesus' ancestry is traced back through him to Abraham and yet according to Matthew, he is not Jesus' father. Joseph was referred to as Mary's husband even though they were not actually married but engaged. At the time, being engaged or betrothed to someone was as binding as marriage.

The point of this is that when Joseph discovered that Mary was expecting a child who was not his, he would have had a right under the law to divorce her. The story tells us a lot about his character and God's purposes:

- He was kind – he decided to divorce Mary quietly so as not to bring her into public disgrace.
- He listened to God – in a dream, an angel told him not to divorce Mary because God had intervened in their lives and the child Mary was carrying was no ordinary child, but conceived by the Holy Spirit.
- He trusted and obeyed God – he did what the angel said and married Mary but in name only until after the baby was born. He called the baby 'Jesus' as he had been told.

●● Think and write . . .

1 How does Matthew show that he believes Jesus is the Messiah?
2 What does 'Incarnation' mean in this context?
3 What is the link between the Fall and Jesus' birth?
4 What does the story tell us about Joseph?

●● Digging deeper

5 What is meant by the phrase 'virgin birth'?
6 Explain the role of the Holy Spirit in the birth of Jesus.
7 Explain why Joseph did not divorce Mary.
8 Explain what the story teaches about God.

●●● Activity

9 Make a poster to show the relationship between Mary, Joseph, God and Jesus.

→ POSSIBLE APPLICATIONS
- Christmas celebrations (page 84)
- materialism (page 84).

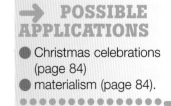

understand

apply

Christmas in the 21st century

Christmas is the biggest and most lavish Christian festival of the year.
Everyone looks forward to it and shops prepare for it months ahead.
Schools stage nativity plays and practise carols for the carol service at the
end of term. We buy presents for our families and friends. At home our
parents spend hours preparing for the invasion of relatives, some more
welcome than others, and making sure there is enough food to last for a
week. We go to, and give Christmas parties where adults often drink too
much and children usually eat too much. In the run-up to Christmas in
2009, people in Britain spent over £4 billion with an average cost per
family for Christmas Day of £725, and that didn't include the presents!

Since Christmas began with a baby in a manger, angels, shepherds
and wise men, everything else must have been added afterwards. Many
people think we have gone so far from the spirit of Christmas that we
have forgotten what it really means. They say that it has become so
commercialised that it is all about material things rather than God. Others
say that the joy and richness of the season help us remember a good and
loving God. Giving presents reminds us of God's gift of his son, and also
the gifts the wise men brought to Jesus. Christmas boxes were
traditionally given to the poor on Boxing Day, hence the name. Today
many charities such as the Salvation Army and Children in Need, work
overtime at Christmas and celebrities often host charity events like Crisis
to raise money for the poor and disadvantaged.

△ Christmas shopping in Oxford Street, London.

△ The custom of sending cards at Christmas started in Queen Victoria's reign. This is the first Christmas card to be mass produced. John Calcott Horsley designed it and John Thompson made it. Today many cards are sold for charity, which continues the tradition of giving to the poor at Christmas.

●●● Activities

1 Make a timetable for Christmas Day for a typical Christian family.
2 Research the work of one of the big charities that operate at Christmas.

●● Think and write . . .

3 Look at A. It is Christmas Eve. What sort of things might be going through the minds of the shoppers?
4 Look at B. What does it say about the spirit of Christmas?
5 How important are presents at Christmas? Explain your answer.
6 Draw two columns in your book. Head one: Positive things about Christmas, and the other: Negative things about Christmas. In the first column, make a list of the things you like and are good about Christmas. In the second column, make a list of those things you don't like or are not so good about Christmas.

●● Digging deeper

7 Do you think we spend too much at Christmas? Give your reasons and show that you have thought of more than one point of view.
8 Is Christmas more about giving or receiving? Explain your answer, showing that you have thought about more than one point of view.

13

The temptations of Jesus

encounter

understand

●● Starter

Is it easier to resist temptation when on your own or when you are with friends?

▽ When the people were being baptised, Jesus was baptised too. As he was praying, heaven was opened and the Holy Spirit descended on him in bodily form like a dove. And a voice came from heaven: 'You are my Son, whom I love; with you I am well pleased.'

'I SAW THE HEAVENS TORN OPEN, AND THE HOLY SPIRIT DESCEND ON JESUS LIKE A DOVE!'

AND SO JESUS WAS BAPTIZED IN THE RIVER JORDAN.

WHEN ASKED ABOUT IT LATER, JOHN DESCRIBED IT IN THESE WORDS:

'I SAW HEAVEN **OPEN**. A VOICE CRIED OUT ~ '

THIS IS MY SON, WHOM I LOVE; WITH HIM I AM WELL PLEASED !

'HE IS THE LAMB OF GOD, COME TO TAKE AWAY THE SINS OF THE WHOLE **WORLD** ! I SAY IN TRUTH, THAT THIS MAN IS THE LIVING **SON OF GOD** !'

I AM SO HUNGRY. LORD GOD, PLEASE HELP ME WITH THIS HUNGER. THE PAIN IS TOO MUCH...

YOU? **HUNGRY** ? WHY, JESUS, IF YOU'RE THE SON OF GOD, WHY DON'T YOU COMMAND THE STONES TO BECOME BREAD ?

YOU KNOW THEY WILL. YOU KNOW HOW **GOOD** THEY'LL TASTE.

DO IT. DO IT **NOW** !

IT IS WRITTEN: 'MAN DOESN'T LIVE ON BREAD ALONE, BUT BY THE WORDS THAT COME FROM GOD'S MOUTH.' THEREFORE I WON'T USE GOD'S POWER FOR MY OWN NEEDS.

▷ After he was baptised, Jesus went into the desert to fast and pray about the best way to do the job God had sent him to do. He would not eat for 40 days.

Read the whole story in **Luke 4**.

Read the whole story in **Luke 4**.

●● Discuss

a) What would have happened if Jesus had given in to the temptations?

b) Why do you think Jesus relied on Scripture to get him through the temptations?

c) In pairs, think about a time when you had to make a decision, which involved a hard but 'right' way and a temptingly easy but 'wrong' way.
   What did you do?

●●● Activity

Divide your page into three sections and draw a picture to show each temptation and how Jesus overcame it. The drawing does not have to be good – you can do stick people if you like – but they must show at a glance what the important points are. This is a useful study skill and will help you when it comes to revision.

The temptations of Jesus

Background

△ The Wadi Rum desert, Jordan.

Life is full of highs and lows and Jesus' life was no different. Jesus had not started preaching or performing miracles, yet at his baptism God said he was pleased with him and called him his son. Throughout his life Jesus had a special relationship with God, whom he called 'Father'. Just as people love, trust and obey their earthly fathers, so Jesus loved, trusted and obeyed God. One of Jesus' titles is 'Son of God'.

Baptism symbolised the death of the old self and the start of a new pure self. By being baptised Jesus took his stand with human beings, heard God saying that he was his son and was filled with the power of God through his Holy Spirit. It is a special passage for Christians because the three persons of God were present: God the Father – the voice from the sky, God the Son – Jesus, and God the Holy Spirit – in the form of the dove. The three persons of God are called the TRINITY.

After this, Jesus went into the desert to fast and pray. It was during this time that he must have worked out the principles, which were to govern his actions as the Messiah. Fasting was a well-established tradition among the Jews, as going without food was believed to make you more aware of spiritual things. The time Jesus fasted was 40 days and is thought by many to symbolise the 40 years that the Jewish nation wandered in the desert after escaping from Egypt with Moses.

During this time the devil made three tempting suggestions. According to Jewish mythology, the devil used to be an angel, but he wanted to make himself equal to God and that resulted in his being thrown out of heaven. He is referred to in the Bible as Lucifer or SATAN and is seen as the challenger of goodness and humanity in the world.

understand

1 Turn these stones into bread

The first temptation was for Jesus to use his power for his own benefit. It would have been so easy to do, no one would know, and his doing this one small miracle for himself would hurt no one. Think back to when you studied the story of the Fall. The temptation was to eat the fruit of the tree. Adam could not resist this temptation. For both, it was a question of obedience. This is why Jesus is sometimes called the 'second Adam' because he triumphed where the first Adam failed.

However, this temptation was not just about satisfying his own hunger, it was about providing food for the people. While the Jews were in the desert with Moses, God provided them with manna. It would be easy for Jesus to provide this kind of help for his people. It would have the added attraction of being popular and make it more likely that they would listen to him.

Jesus' reply showed that he knew that the state of people's spiritual lives was as important, if not more so, than their physical lives.

2 All this will be yours if you worship me

The second temptation was to be the kind of Old Testament hero the Jews were used to. It was widely believed that the Messiah would come and save them from their problems. Jewish history is full of stories of freedom fighters and at the time of Jesus a guerrilla group called Zealots, were actively involved in underground resistance to the Romans.

The devil was showing Jesus how he could win over the Jewish people by spectacularly wiping out the Romans and restoring Israel to the Jews. The devil offered to put his own enormous influence on the world at the disposal of Jesus for the promotion of the Messianic Kingdom.

Giving in to this temptation would avoid the necessity of dying on the cross and would win the world by a compromise with evil. Jesus knew this was merely an earthly kingdom and not the one that mattered the most. He also knew that this was not God's way because it would involve employing the devil's tactics to accomplish.

By citing the first of the Ten Commandments, Jesus showed his obedience to God and his trust in him.

3 Throw yourself off the Temple

The third temptation was to show his authority in a dramatic way that would remove any doubt from people's minds that Jesus was who he claimed to be. The Temple was the principal place of worship for the Jews and was situated in Jerusalem. It was a very public place and was always filled with people. The devil also used Psalm 91 to try and persuade him. Note Jesus' reply – 'Do not put the Lord your God to the test' (Deuteronomy 6.16).

People's faith had to be based on absolute trust in God and not proved to them by miraculous stunts, however good the cause might be. It effectively silenced the devil.

●● Think and write ...

1 Plot Jesus' highs and lows in this story on a simple graph.
2 Make a wall chart of the different ways everyone in your class has been tempted. Draw a graph or bar chart to show the most common temptations.
3 Look back at the drawings you made of Jesus' temptations. Add to each one the reason it was important that Jesus resisted it.

●● Digging deeper

4 Look at some of the people in Section 3 of this book, such as Jackie Pullinger and Mother Teresa. Write a short paragraph describing the kinds of temptations they may have had to overcome.

→ POSSIBLE APPLICATIONS

● resisting temptation at school and work (page 90)
● the problem of evil (TRB unit 2).

understand

apply

●● **Discuss**

What is a conscience and why do we have one?

Lead us not into temptation . . .

Just as Jesus was tempted to do the wrong things in his life, so in today's world we are surrounded by temptation:

to eat too much

to cheat on someone

to gossip about or punch someone

to take something that isn't ours

to tell a lie

to spend too much money

WE ARE TEMPTED ...

to do nothing and so allow something we know is wrong to happen

to take dangerous or illegal short cuts to achieve something

to drink alcohol when underage or take drugs

Everyone has their weaknesses and what is difficult to resist for one person is no problem for another. People are tempted in different ways in different stages of their lives. For example, at school a pupil might be tempted to run in the corridor or talk after lights out; something irrelevant for an adult. But what about temptations that aren't exactly wrong, or are so widely practised as to be normal?

Here are three people – a schoolgirl, a businessman, and an athlete.

Lisa is fifteen and working for her GCSEs. She would like to get straight As but the coursework is very time consuming and rather hard. Her older sister has offered to lend her the Geography coursework she did for GCSE and for which she got an A grade. It would mean Lisa wouldn't have to go out and do all the research, so she could spend more time on her other subjects. No one would find out about it…

Richard is 37 and an up-and-coming manager in his company. He wants to push his career up a notch and has on his desk details of a brilliant idea. The idea comes from a bright young junior in his firm and Richard is tempted to do a careful bit of editing and pass it off as his own. The Board of Directors would be impressed and the magic door to the boardroom might open for him. Passing off, as this practice is known, happens all the time and no doubt the junior would be annoyed, but he'd have other opportunities…

Andy is an athlete and hopes to be picked for the Olympic team. He knows that some athletes take performance-enhancing drugs and get away with it. Some of his professional friends have advised him to take certain steps to improve his performance, even if it is only an autologous blood transfusion, in which he would take his own blood in advance and then replace it shortly before the race. This would give him more oxygen enabling him to run faster. He is very tempted because it might just make that difference and it isn't exactly a drug…

● ● Think and write . . .

1 Read the temptations facing Lisa, Richard and Andy. What might they decide to do if their decision is based on:
   a) their religious convictions?
   b) who they are?
   c) the law of the land?
   d) whether it will hurt someone?
2 How are Lisa's, Richard's and Andy's situations similar?
3 How are they different?

● ● Digging deeper

4 'The end always justifies the means.' Do you agree? Give your reasons.
5 Imagine you are one of the three people above. Write an imaginary conversation you might have with yourself as you wrestle with your conscience.

14 Jesus and the outcasts

encounter

●● Starter

Discuss:
1 What kind of people would Jesus have associated with if he had been living in today's world?
2 Why would he have associated with these particular people?

As you read the stories, think about what they have in common.

A

Read **Luke 19.1–10** – the story of Zacchaeus.

1 What do you think Zacchaeus is thinking in this painting?
2 From what you know from reading the story, what do you think the people under the tree are saying to each other?

understand

△ An African representation of Jesus speaking to Zacchaeus. Which character do you think is Zacchaeus? Which is Jesus?

B

Read **Luke 7.36–50** – the story of Jesus, the woman and Simon the Pharisee.

△ This picture of the woman wiping Jesus' feet with her hair is by a French painter.

Jesus told Simon this parable:

41'Two men owed money to a certain money-lender. One owed him five hundred denarii, and the other fifty. 42Neither of them had the money to pay him back, so he cancelled the debts of both. Now which of them will love him more?'

43Simon replied, 'I suppose the one who had the biggest debt cancelled.'

'You have judged correctly,' Jesus said.

44Then he turned towards the woman and said to Simon, 'Do you see this woman? I came into your house. You did not give me any water for my feet, but she wet my feet with her tears and wiped them with her hair. 45You did not give me a kiss, but this woman, from the time I entered, has not stopped kissing my feet. 46You did not put oil on my head, but she has poured perfume on my feet. 47Therefore, I tell you, her many sins have been forgiven – for she loved much. But he who has been forgiven little loves little.'

Luke 7.41–47.

1 Look closely at the guests round the table in this painting. Which one do you think is Simon the Pharisee?
2 What did Jesus' story mean?
3 How did the woman's actions show her faith?

Jesus and the outcasts

A

Zacchaeus

Tax collectors in first-century Palestine were not paid; they simply collected as much money as they could so that they could have a good sum left over for themselves. This is what Zacchaeus was doing in Jericho.

Jesus invited himself to Zacchaeus' house before Zacchaeus changed his ways. The crowd would have been shocked, because to eat in a man's house was to accept that man and everyone knew he was not accepted in society. The word 'SINNER' here means outcast. Zacchaeus was a changed man as a result. Note what he did:

● He said sorry.
● He promised to pay back what he had stolen.
● He offered to pay compensation to his victims of four times the amount he had taken from them.

Jesus said that Salvation had come to Zacchaeus' house. Salvation means being saved, in this case it meant Zacchaeus being saved from a life outside God's love because of the kind of life he had been leading.

It was not being ostracised that made him change his ways (if that had been the case, he would have stopped cheating long before). It was through being accepted as a true son of Abraham (Luke 19.9), that very rich ancestor of his who first had faith. Abraham displayed that faith in his actions, just as Zacchaeus was now doing.

● ● **Think and write . . .**

1 Why were tax collectors hated?
2 Why were the crowd shocked when Jesus went to Zacchaeus' house?
3 What changed in Zacchaeus' life after he met Jesus?

● ● **Digging deeper**

4 What did Jesus mean when he said, 'Today salvation has come to this house'?
5 How did Zacchaeus show faith in Jesus?

B

Jesus, the woman and Simon the Pharisee

On this occasion Jesus is again at a meal but this time as the guest of a Pharisee named Simon. Simon may have wanted to question Jesus about his teaching in order to find out if he really were a prophet sent from God.

Then a woman with a very bad reputation came in off the street and started kissing Jesus' feet and wiping them with her hair. Finally she poured perfume over his feet and all this time Jesus did nothing to stop her.

Simon came to the conclusion that Jesus could not be a prophet after all or he would surely know exactly what kind of woman was paying him all this attention, and stop her.

Jesus told Simon a parable that showed everyone at the table that he not only knew about the woman's past but forgave her because she showed faith in Jesus.

Simon was embarrassed by the story because it showed him up in a bad light. As Jesus pointed out, he had not extended even the commonest courtesy of washing his feet before they sat down to eat, let alone pouring olive oil on his head as befitted an honoured guest.

The other people at the table asked each other about who Jesus might be that he was able to forgive sins.

Jesus pointed out, as on many other occasions, that it was her faith that had saved her.

●● Think and write . . .

6 Explain why Simon the Pharisee was critical of Jesus in this story.
7 How did Jesus' story show Simon in a bad light?
8 Why did people wonder who Jesus was?

●● Digging deeper

9 Explain why the religious leaders were critical of Jesus.
10 How are both this story and the story of Zachaeus about faith and love?

●●● Activity

6 Choose one of the characters and write a before and after description of them.

⟶ POSSIBLE APPLICATIONS

● who helps today's outcasts (page 96)
● prejudice and racial discrimination (page 122)
● the example of Mother Teresa (page 138), Jackie Pullinger (page 140), Martin Luther King (page 40) and Trevor Huddleston (page 34).

Who are today's outcasts?

●● Discuss

a) How is this story like the stories on pages 94–95?

Some years ago, a single mother was living in the London Docklands area. At the time, having children without being married made her a social outcast. She went to a women's meeting at her local church and enjoyed it, so she went back every week, taking her baby with her. After a while, the vicar told her not to come again or the other women would stop coming. Fortunately, the **Salvation Army** found her and helped her to develop her faith.

The Salvation Army still works among social outcasts today. Their aim is to show Christ's love by caring for others.

> We put faith into practice. We promise, for Christ's sake, to care for the poor, feed the hungry, clothe the naked, love the unlovable and befriend the friendless.

The Salvation Army runs projects that help people to rediscover their self-respect and many of them also find faith in God. These three stories are adapted from their website, www.salvationarmy.org.uk.

Helping the homeless

The Salvation Army helps homeless people by providing food and shelter for people who live on the streets. The aim is not just to give them somewhere to sleep but to help them face and overcome the problems that put them on the streets in the first place. By being offered this kind of help, homeless people can start to build new lives for themselves.

Alex's story I'm sixteen and was homeless when the Salvation Army gave me a place in a Lifehouse centre for homeless young people. I've been there three months and it's alright. The best thing is feeling safe, away from gangs and fights. The staff are really nice and help me with college where I am doing a diploma. I've learnt a lot being here especially in the life skills classes where we discuss important issues such as sexual health and budgeting. I've even learnt to cook and can communicate with people better. My ambition now is to be a pilot. The Salvation Army turned my life around.

understand

apply

Helping people affected by drug and alcohol misuse

The Salvation Army helps addicts to overcome their initial addiction and re-establishes them into the community and into their families. It runs rehabilitation centres and supports the families of the people it helps.

John's story My name is John and I was a heavy drinker. I drank to get drunk. I got into fights and started gambling. It is weird that something as superficial as alcohol can ruin your life. I became homeless and started to go to the Salvation Army's soup kitchen at night for a hot meal. My whole life changed when I started attending the New Futures workshop. The love, care and time they lavished on me was amazing.

I studied some of the subjects I missed at school. I made new friends and started going to Salvation Army services on Sundays. One Sunday I gave my life to God and asked him to help me with my alcohol addiction.

Helping people who have been in prison

Many prisons in the UK have Salvation Army chaplains who visit prisoners and help them get started in life once they are released. Their ministry is practical and non-judgemental. The Salvation Army also supports the families of people they help in prison.

Paul's story After I had been in the prison about a week, a Salvation Army officer opened my cell door and said my mother had asked him to visit me. He never tried to preach to me, although he knew when to just talk and when to pray with me. That was over six years ago. Today I live a quiet life, I have found peace at last.

●● Discuss

b) What is it about the homeless, drug addicts and alcoholics that makes people avoid them?

c) How can ordinary people help these social outcasts?

d) People with disabilities used to be social outcasts. What has changed?

●● Think and write ...

1 How does the Salvation Army help
   a) the homeless
   b) drug addicts and alcoholics
   c) people with a criminal record?
2 Suggest two ways you could help one of the groups of people mentioned in this unit.
3 Describe how the Salvation Army helped one of the people whose stories are told in this unit.

●● Digging deeper

4 Why should Christians in particular help such people?

Jesus' Life,
Death and
Resurrection;
Jesus'
Teaching

15

Being a
follower of
Jesus

key question

What does it
mean to be a
follower of
Jesus?

encounter

●● Starter

Imagine your favourite pop star has announced he/she is setting up a brand new community of all his/her fans. She/he will be in charge. All members of the community will have to do what the pop star orders. Think of reasons why you might join/not join the community.

●●● Activity

1 The first story in this unit has been set out as a radio play. Add your own sound effects and record it.

understand

△ A modern fisherman on the Sea of Galilee.

Narrator: Jesus attracted people who liked to listen to him telling them stories. However, most of them didn't really understand what it meant to follow Jesus. In this play, Jesus shows how his disciples must be: obedient, willing to give up everything they have, and willing to serve others.

Read the full story in **Luke 5.1–11**.

On the shores of the Sea of Galilee

Jesus: Hi, Pete! Can we push this boat further out? Let's go fishing.

Simon Peter: Actually, mate, me and the lads worked all night and caught nothing . . . not a sausage. But seeing as how you ask us, we'll give it another whirl. *(shouts)* Guys! Oy, Johnny, Jamie! Give us a hand. We're going out again.

Simon Peter: Right . . . that's far enough. Chuck us the end of that rope, John.

James: On the count of three then, lads! One . . . two . . . three . . .

John: Will you look at this! I've never seen so many fish.

Simon Peter: Wow! Double wow!

John: Er . . . looks like we've caught a fish or two.

James: Guys – we're very low in the water. Can we get back to the shore a.s.a.p?

John: *(shouting to other boat)* You look like you're in the same boat. Better hurry!

Man from other boat: Ha ha! Very funny. This lot'll put food into my kids' mouths for a long time. Good tip off I'd say!

Simon Peter: I don't think I can handle this. Jesus, mate, I'm only a humble guy. I'm . . . like . . . not a particularly good sort of bloke. You'd be better off not hanging around people like me.

Jesus: Believe me, Peter, forget the fish; from now on you'll be catching men!

B Jesus and the rich man

¹⁷As Jesus started on his way, a man ran up to him and fell on his knees before him. 'Good teacher,' he asked, 'what must I do to inherit eternal life?'

¹⁸'Why do you call me good?' Jesus answered. 'No one is good – except God alone. ¹⁹You know the commandments: "Do not murder, do not commit adultery, do not steal, do not give false testimony, do not defraud, honour your father and mother."'

²⁰'Teacher,' he declared, 'all these I have kept since I was a boy.'

²¹Jesus looked at him and loved him. 'One thing you lack,' he said. 'Go, sell everything you have and give to the poor, and you will have treasure in heaven. Then come, follow me.'

²²At this the man's face fell. He went away sad, because he had great wealth.

²³Jesus looked around and said to his disciples, 'How hard it is for the rich to enter the kingdom of God!'

²⁴The disciples were amazed at his words. But Jesus said again, 'Children, how hard it is to enter the kingdom of God! ²⁵It is easier for a camel to go through the eye of a needle than for a rich man to enter the kingdom of God.'

²⁶The disciples were even more amazed, and said to each other, 'Who then can be saved?'

²⁷Jesus looked at them and said, 'With man this is impossible, but not with God; all things are possible with God.'

²⁸Peter said to him, 'We have left everything to follow you!'

²⁹'I tell you the truth,' Jesus replied, 'no one who has left home or brothers or sisters or mother or father or children or fields for me and the gospel ³⁰will fail to receive a hundred times as much in this present age (homes, brothers, sisters, mothers, children and fields – and with them, persecutions) and in the age to come, eternal life. ³¹But many who are first will be last, and the last first.'

Mark 10.17–31.

● ● ● **Activity**

2 Write a radio play about this second story.

● ● **Discuss**

What do both these stories have to say about following Jesus?

Being a follower of Jesus

Jesus calls the first disciples

A **disciple** is someone who follows a teacher and tries to live according to that teaching. Jesus eventually had twelve disciples and this story is about how he 'called' the first ones. The word 'call' is a special one and Christians often talk about being 'called' by God to do something. They feel that God has asked them to do a specific job, just as Jesus asked his disciples to a job for him.

Jesus often stood in a boat to speak to large crowds. It probably gave him some space and enabled everyone to hear what he had to say. Lake Gennesaret is also called the Sea of Galilee. After he had finished teaching the people, it was time to teach those who would become his close disciples. Even at this early stage Simon Peter recognised Jesus' authority because he agreed to let down the nets again even though they had caught nothing all night. He said, 'But because you say so I will let down the nets' (verse 5).

The miraculous catch of fish they caught as a result of doing what Jesus said made Simon realise that Jesus was someone with a close relationship with God. It made him deeply aware of his own sinful nature and shortcomings. That is why he fell to his knees and asked Jesus to go away, but Jesus told him not to be afraid because he had important work for him to do: being a 'fisher' of people.

This was not the first time these fishermen had been with Jesus but their rather loose association with him now became a closely knit unit. They were amazed by what had happened and this led them to follow the man who could work such a miracle.

Simon Peter learnt some valuable lessons:

1 Obedience to Jesus got results.
2 Jesus was a miracle worker.
3 Despite his own inadequacy as a person, Jesus could still make something of him.

Note one last thing about the story: look at verse 11. Here were the nets full to bursting with fish, still in the boats and representing a colossal sum of money. The men left them and followed Jesus. They realised their priorities had changed.

△ A scene from the film *Jesus of Nazareth* showing Jesus talking to fishermen who would become his disciples.

● ● Discuss

a) What does it mean to have a CALLING?

● ● Think and write ...

1 What is a disciple?
2 Why did the disciples change their minds about letting their nets down again?
3 What did Jesus mean by saying he would make Simon a fisher of men?

● ● Digging deeper

4 Why was Simon Peter afraid after they had caught so much fish?
5 What does this story tell us about Simon Peter?
6 What do we learn about discipleship from this story?

The rich young man

- The first thing Jesus did was to try and stop him getting carried away on the tide of enthusiasm and emotion, without counting the cost of being a follower.
- He said the way to life was by keeping the Commandments. Note that the man brushed this suggestion aside, saying that he'd done all that, so he must have had quite a depth of spiritual understanding. Unfortunately, he lacked the strength of character to take the next step.

How wealth was understood in first-century Israel

- Wealth was seen as a reward from God for leading a good life.
- Wealth was a status symbol. The man probably had the first-century equivalent of a private jet and a yacht in the Bahamas.
- It was believed that being wealthy would make it easier for someone to get to heaven.

This kind of enthusiastic person was exactly who Jesus needed to have around him and to become a disciple, but he recognised the hold the man's wealth had over him. He wanted to trust God, but he needed a back-up just in case.

It was a shock to the disciples as well because they thought the rich man would be streets ahead of them on the road to heaven.

Jesus had to explain to them that no one had a head start on the road to heaven.

Jesus' conversation with the disciples afterwards pointed out that leaving family and worldly possessions in order to serve God would bring a reward even in this life, and a greater one in heaven. He explained that the Kingdom placed values on spiritual wealth, which lasts, following Jesus' teaching and obeying God. In contrast the world values gold and material possessions, which do not last.

●● Think and write ...

7 Why did the rich young man think he would be able to follow Jesus?

8 Why was he unable to become a disciple after all?

9 Why were the disciples dismayed by what Jesus said to the rich young man?

●● Digging deeper

10 What does this story teach about discipleship?

11 In what ways might great wealth get in the way of following Jesus' teaching today?

12 What did Jesus mean when he said, 'Many who are first will be last, and the last first'?

●● Discuss

b) Can a person be a Christian and be wealthy?

→ POSSIBLE APPLICATIONS

- wealth and possessions (TRB unit 15)
- changing priorities: how does a person serve God today? (page 102).

Changing priorities

▷ Guy Brooking discussing his next mission.

B The best place to be

The challenges of mission life leave Guy and Gail Brooking and their four children undeterred – they are convinced they are where they should be.

A fascination for flying and a calling to be involved in mission work had always been Guy Brooking's twin passions. His ambition to combine them was realised when he started to work for Mission Aviation Fellowship (MAF). The Brookings sold their home to pay for flying lessons, after which they had only £50 left. They believed that God would help them.

Now they live in Nairobi and Guy trains pilots in Kenya, Tanzania, Uganda and Mongolia.

'I find myself stretched in many different directions,' he says. 'It has caused us to question our role here, and even our whole future. But we are reminded of our calling to mission, and particularly to MAF. That doesn't mean the difficulties get any easier – but it does mean we know we are in the place God wants us.'

Regular flights into southern Sudan are a reminder of the vital importance of the work in which Guy plays such a major part. He has flown an eye team from Christian Blind Mission to remote locations in Kenya, Somalia and southern Sudan, enabling medical work to be carried out far away from civilisation. Guy made several emergency flights out of Dodoma after the worst rail disaster in Tanzania, ferrying victims to hospital.

On another occasion he flew a large quantity of vaccine to help quell a whooping cough outbreak in Kimatong, southern Sudan.

The icy blast of Mongolia and the searing heat of Africa are all part and parcel of Guy's work and calling. But the family would be nowhere else because for them, it is where God wants them to be.

Adapted from *MAF News*, September–November 2004.

apply

Since this article was written, Guy Brooking has a new job in New Zealand. He said, 'Whilst we no longer work for a missionary organisation, we still feel called to be serving God, and I really believe that God can use you whoever you are, wherever you are and in whatever you are doing.'

△ Guy and Gail Brooking with their children.

△ Guy Brooking checking his plane before a flight.

●● Think and write ...

1 What makes people like the Brookings give up everything and go and work for God abroad?
2 What steps did Guy and his wife have to take before his dream became a reality?
3 Look at picture D. How can Guy help people in remote areas?

●● Digging deeper

4 Guy Brooking talked about his 'calling to mission work'. What did he mean?
5 What do you think is the most important issue for the Brookings? Give your reasons.
6 Do you have to work for a missionary organisation in order to serve God? Give reasons for your answer.

encounter

● ● Starter

Discuss: If a new person joined your class and became more popular than you overnight, how would you react to them?

● ● Think and write ...

1 How did the friends show their persistence?
2 Why did the scribes criticise Jesus?
3 How did Jesus answer them?

Flow charts are a good way to summarise a story.

Read **Mark 2.1–12**.

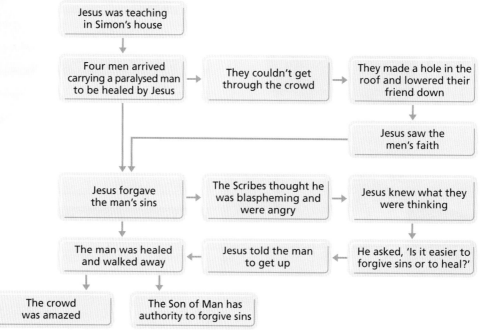

Jesus was teaching in Simon's house

→

Four men arrived carrying a paralysed man to be healed by Jesus → They couldn't get through the crowd → They made a hole in the roof and lowered their friend down

Jesus saw the men's faith

Jesus forgave the man's sins → The Scribes thought he was blaspheming and were angry → Jesus knew what they were thinking

The man was healed and walked away ← Jesus told the man to get up ← He asked, 'Is it easier to forgive sins or to heal?'

The crowd was amazed

The Son of Man has authority to forgive sins

A Jesus calms the storm

³⁵That day when evening came, he said to his disciples, 'Let us go over to the other side.' ³⁶Leaving the crowd behind, they took him along, just as he was, in the boat. There were also other boats with him. ³⁷A furious squall came up, and the waves broke over the boat, so that it was nearly swamped. ³⁸Jesus was in the stern, sleeping on a cushion. The disciples woke him and said to him, 'Teacher, don't you care if we drown?'

³⁹He got up, rebuked the wind and said to the waves, 'Quiet! Be still!' Then the wind died down and it was completely calm.

⁴⁰He said to his disciples, 'Why are you so afraid? Do you still have no faith?'

⁴¹They were terrified and asked each other, 'Who is this? Even the wind and the waves obey him!'

Mark 4.35–41.

△ *Jesus calming the storm* by He Qi.

●● Think and write ...

4 Describe what happened when Jesus took the disciples out in the boat.

5 When the disciples woke Jesus, what did they expect him to do?

6 Why were they afraid once everything had calmed down?

●● Digging deeper

7 Why did Jesus question the disciples' faith?

8 What does this story reveal about who Jesus is?

●●● Activity

9 You are a reporter with the *Galilee Gazette* and you hear about the amazing story of a man controlling the weather. Interview one of the disciples on the boat about what happened. Put in a 'photograph' of one of the people involved, and a picture showing what the Sea of Galilee can be like in a storm. Choose a dramatic title for your article.

understand

⬤ ⬤ Discuss

a) Do you think people's illnesses are ever caused by sin?

b) Is it ever right to go against authority?

▷ A nineteenth-century artist's interpretation of Jesus laying hands on a paralysed man. According to the Gospel writers, once word got out that Jesus healed people, everywhere he went the sick were brought to him and he healed many people.

⬤ ⬤ Think and write ...

1 What part did faith play in this story?

2 Explain why the Scribes were angry with Jesus.

3 What did Jesus show about himself by forgiving the man's sins and healing him?

⬤ ⬤ Digging deeper

4 What was behind the concern shown by the Scribes?

5 Why do you think Jesus forgave the man's sins before healing him?

A miracle is a happening that cannot be fully explained by natural events or human reason. The miracles of Jesus need to be seen in the light of his divine power and in his purpose in the world, which is salvation.

Jesus heals the paralysed man

This is a dramatic story and one which raises several interesting points.

● It was the faith of the four friends rather than that of the man himself, that led to his being healed. Faith is having an active trust in someone or something. Nearly all the other healing miracles required the faith of the person needing healing.

● Jesus' first action was to forgive the man for his sin. Christians believe that sin is something that cuts people off from God. It can be a wrong attitude as well as bad actions or words. By forgiving the man's sins, Jesus showed his care for people's spiritual health as well as their physical well-being.

● Jesus caused an angry reaction from the Scribes. They followed Jesus around on purpose to try and catch him out. Popularity was regarded with suspicion and fear – 'Who is this man? What is his authority? He's not one of us ...'. The Scribes believed that only God could forgive sins, so when Jesus forgave the man, they said it was BLASPHEMY – speaking against God or making yourself equal to God. Jesus' action marked the beginning of the conflict between himself and the religious authorities.

● Jesus' reply to the Scribes' question proved his authority to forgive sins because he told the man to get up and walk, which the man did. If, as most people believed, God had sent his paralysis as a punishment, God must have forgiven him if he could now walk.

Jesus calms the storm

● ● Discuss

c) In both these miracles, Jesus is dealing with spiritual problems as well as physical ones. Is one more important for well-being than the other?

If you had been a Jew living in first-century Israel, you would have had a very healthy respect for the sea and large expanses of water in general. You would have grown up with the belief that evil spirits lived in the sea and in the deep waters under the earth. If you earned your living by fishing, you would also have experienced the sudden squalls that blow up and know how easily your boat could be capsized. If you put both thoughts together, a rough sea was a terrifying thing. The spirits were coming up to the surface and attacking you, and at any moment you could be thrown into the water and drown. This story therefore is about more than Jesus' authority over nature; it is about his authority over the spirit world too. The way he said 'Be still!' was like the way he cast out evil spirits.

Going out in a boat is always a risky business but such was Jesus' trust in God, he was able to sleep peacefully, even through a storm. Mark adds the detail that he was asleep in the stern, that is, the back of the boat, with his head on a cushion. This was probably the wooden or leather rower's seat. This story shows both Jesus' humanity – he was exhausted so he slept – and his deity – the fact that the wind and the waves obeyed him.

There is yet another way of looking at this story and that is to see it as a message of peace to the persecuted Church of the first century. The stormy waves are a symbol for the troubles the Church was experiencing at the time in which Mark was writing his gospel. The disciples were doing what God wanted them to do but obedience does not mean they will not go through hard times. The disciples were frightened of the storm and indignant that Jesus should sleep through the danger. They needed to be reminded just as the early Christians did, that Jesus was both with them and in control, and that they should have faith through their difficulties. The resulting calm after the storm represents true peace that God's triumph over evil brings.

● ● Think and write . . .

6 Why were people afraid of the sea at the time of Jesus?
7 Why was Jesus asleep?
8 What does the story teach about Jesus? Give evidence from the passage for each observation.
9 What do we learn about the disciples?

● ● Digging deeper

10 How might this story help the early Christians who read it?
11 In what ways can this event be seen as a miracle?
12 What does this story teach about faith?

→ POSSIBLE APPLICATIONS

● healing (page 109)
● ministry to the sick and dying, such as the work of the hospice movement (page 142)
● Jackie Pullinger and her drug rehabilitation centres (page 140)
● Mother Teresa and the care and prayer she offered the sick, the destitute and the dying (page 138)
● modern miracles (page 108).

Do miracles happen today?

△ Passengers step out of the aircraft onto the wings of Flight 1549.

On 16 January 2009, the US Airways Airbus A320 crash landed in the Hudson River just minutes after take off. This particular stretch of water runs through Manhattan with skyscrapers on either side. The pilot, Captain Chesley Sullenberger, managed to ditch the plane after its engines were disabled by a flock of geese, without any loss of life. There were no boats in its path when normally there would have been many carrying tourists photographing the famous Manhattan skyline. As soon as it landed several water taxis rushed to its aid and all 155 passengers and crew, including a baby, were safely evacuated before the aircraft sank. The only significant injury was to someone who broke both legs; all other injuries were minor.

As the aeroplane came in low over the river and it became clear they were going to crash, many people on board started praying. One of the passengers was Jeff Kolodjay. He said that he heard a loud bang and the plane filled with smoke. 'It was pretty scary, man. We got out by the luck of God. I take my hat off to the pilot – it was incredible we all made it off.'

The survival of all on board seems to have been due to a number of things: the skill of the pilot, immediate help from nearby boats, the fact that the door opened easily and that no one panicked but just stepped out and walked calmly along the wings to await rescue. The Governor of New York State called it 'Miracle on the Hudson'.

Travelling to be healed

Some places have a tradition of healing. The shrine at Lourdes is a famous Catholic healing centre in France and thousands flock there hoping to be healed. While they are there they receive the laying on of hands, prayer and counselling. The director of the centre is Patrick Theillier and he describes Lourdes as a 'laboratory of healing'.

While healing is occasionally physical, many more people experience emotional and spiritual healing. Theillier thinks that of the seven thousand cures reported to the Lourdes medical bureau, over two thousand of them defy medical explanation.

One example of a healing at Lourdes is a man called Joseph Charpentier, who had been in a wheelchair for nineteen years. During the service he was anointed with oil and prayed for. He said that he felt a 'great warmth rise from my feet to my heart'. He was able to get out of his wheelchair and return home.

Although everyone in his home village was amazed, not all were convinced that a miracle had happened. The priest himself said that he wouldn't say it was a miracle even though it was extraordinary. A specialist doctor thought that Joseph might have been unable to walk because of a psychological disorder, so no actual physical healing had taken place.

It all depends on how one defines a miracle. Many would argue that a miracle had indeed taken place, even if the illness had started in the mind.

●● Think and write ...

1 Why did the State Governor call the rescue of Flight 1549 a miracle?
2 Why did the passengers on the aircraft start praying?
3 What is offered at Lourdes that makes people go there?
4 Do services of healing fulfil a useful purpose? Give your reasons.

●● Digging deeper

5 'There is more than one kind of healing.' Do you agree? Give your reasons.
6 Do the sceptics (who believe we should seek rational explanations for apparently miraculous events) have a valid point? State your reasons.

△ Pilgrims gather in Lourdes.

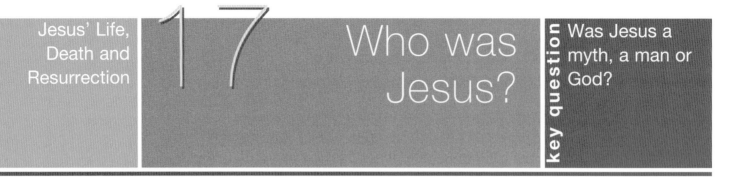

encounter

understand

apply

● ● Starter

Take a class vote: do you think Jesus was a myth, just a good man, or God?

Conversation at Caesarea Philippi

The account you are about to read is written as Peter might have recounted the conversation. You will need to read the full story in **Mark 8.27–33**. Caesarea Philippi in those days was a city; today you can only see the ruins. The source of the River Jordan was close by.

A The day we went to Caesarea Philippi stands out in my mind as one of the most significant days in my life. I had been with Jesus for a while and watched him heal the sick, forgive people their sins, feed a crowd and countless other things. I had also heard him speak on many occasions and a conviction was growing in me that Jesus, my friend, was someone really special. My country has waited so long for a Messiah to save us like Moses did, and Joshua, and all my heroes.

On this particular day, Jesus had just given a blind man his sight back and we were headed out to the villages near Caesarea Philippi. On the way, Jesus suddenly asked us who people were saying he was. Well, there were all kinds of rumours going round and we told him what those were. He was John the Baptist come back from the grave. He was Elijah. He was a prophet.

He was silent for a while, then he asked us directly who we thought he was. I was so sure then, that he really was the Messiah, that I came right out with it and told him. 'Don't tell anyone about me,' was what he said. So I was right all along!

Jesus then started to talk about the Son of Man and we knew he must be speaking about himself, but none of it made any sense. He said he must suffer and be rejected by the elders, the chief priests and the teachers of the Law, but I can't see why that should happen if he's the Messiah. Then he said he would be put to death but rise again three days later. I didn't take much notice of that second bit at the time; I was too concerned about the way he was talking about dying. I tried to show him that there was no need to go as far as dying. Everyone knew he had power and once they understood he was the Messiah, they would all be on his side cheering him on.

Jesus' reaction stunned me. He looked at me and said, 'Get away, Satan!' I could not believe he was talking to me. Then he told me that my thoughts did not come from God but from the world. I tell you, I've never forgotten those words.

▷ Caesarea Philippi, where Peter made his famous declaration that Jesus was the Messiah. This nearby cave contains the source of a stream that flows into the River Jordan and the area was a place of pagan worship. The niches you can see in the rock were for statues of the god Pan. It is significant that Jesus chose this spot: he was challenging the worship of pagan gods and predicting the spread of the Gospel.

The Transfiguration

C ²After six days Jesus took Peter, James and John with him and led them up a high mountain, where they were all alone. There he was transfigured before them. ³His clothes became dazzling white, whiter than anyone in the world could bleach them. ⁴And there appeared before them Elijah and Moses, who were talking with Jesus.

⁵Peter said to Jesus, 'Rabbi, it is good for us to be here. Let us put up three shelters – one for you, one for Moses and one for Elijah.' ⁶(He did not know what to say, they were so frightened.)

⁷Then a cloud appeared and enveloped them, and a voice came from the cloud: 'This is my Son, whom I love. Listen to him!'

⁸Suddenly, when they looked around, they no longer saw anyone with them except Jesus.

⁹As they were coming down the mountain, Jesus gave them orders not to tell anyone what they had seen until the Son of Man had risen from the dead. ¹⁰They kept the matter to themselves, discussing what 'rising from the dead' meant.

¹¹And they asked him, 'Why do the teachers of the law say that Elijah must come first?'

¹²Jesus replied, 'To be sure, Elijah does come first, and restores all things. Why then is it written that the Son of Man must suffer much and be rejected? ¹³But I tell you, Elijah has come, and they have done to him everything they wished, just as it is written about him.'

Mark 9.2–13.

●● Discuss

Why was this information about Jesus to be secret for the moment?

●●● Activity

Continue Peter's memories and write about how he remembers the Transfiguration.

Who was Jesus?

Peter's declaration about Jesus at Caesarea Philippi

It was time for Jesus to find out who his disciples thought he was, so that he could prepare them for what was to happen.

At the point when Peter made his famous statement of faith – 'You are the Messiah' – what had he seen Jesus do?

- Forgive a man's sins
- Heal the sick, including the deaf, the blind and the lame
- Perform miracles such as feeding the five thousand
- Raise the dead
- Cast out demons
- Teach about the Kingdom of God
- Change people's lives, such as that of Levi the tax collector.

These miracles were linked with the Old Testament prophecies about the Messiah. Peter began to see this, but he did not fully understand what being the Messiah would mean for Jesus. In particular he did not accept the idea of a suffering Messiah. Look back at Unit 13. Jesus recognised Satan tempting him as he had done in the desert. That was why he said 'Get away, Satan!' Peter was not looking at things from God's point of view, but from a human perspective.

Jesus spoke of his suffering and referred to himself as the Son of Man. This idea of a human being with special authority comes from the book of Daniel in the Old Testament (see box, left).

Beliefs about the Messiah

The Messiah is a figure of salvation in the Old Testament. However, he would be human, not divine. The idea of the Messiah being God in human form was blasphemous to all Jews.

The Jews believed three main things about the Messiah:

1 He would be a **Son of David** – David was the greatest king of Israel and his reign was looked on as a golden era. The Messiah would be a descendant of David and a great king like David had been.
2 He would be a **political leader**. The Zealots were a group of freedom fighters and they wanted a military leader to help them overthrow the Roman oppressors.
3 He would be a **spiritual leader** – he would bring in an age of peace. Prophecies such as those in Isaiah 9 and 11 support this belief.

It is not surprising that Jesus asked his disciples to keep quiet for the time being. People would expect a nationalist hero, and follow him in the hopes of seeing the Romans sent packing. They would not understand the concept of a suffering Messiah any more than the disciples did.

---

understand

[13]'In my vision at night I looked, and there before me was one like a son of man, coming with the clouds of heaven. He approached the Ancient of Days, and was led into his presence. [14]He was given authority, glory and sovereign power; all peoples, nations and men of every language worshipped him. His dominion is an everlasting dominion that will not pass away, and his kingdom is one that will never be destroyed.'

Daniel 7.13–14.

●● Discuss

a) Does it really matter whether Jesus was God or not?
b) What would you have felt if you had been present at the Transfiguration?

The Transfiguration

The Transfiguration happened six days after the conversation at Caesarea Philippi. Transfiguration means change of appearance. Jesus' physical appearance was changed and his clothes shone but it was also a spiritual experience for him.

The disciples saw Jesus in a different way. There was something about him that they could not explain and they were filled with awe.

△ Church painting showing the Transfiguration.

The significance of Moses and Elijah

● **Moses** represented the **Law**. He is one of the great Old Testament heroes who merits the title 'Messiah' because he rescued the Jews from slavery in Egypt.
● **Elijah** represented the **Jewish Prophets**. The Prophets were people through whom God communicated with his people. Elijah was the most important of these prophets.

The reaction of the disciples, especially Peter, showed they were completely out of their depth and didn't know what to do. No notice was taken of Peter's suggestion to build a shelter; instead a voice spoke saying, 'This is my son whom I love; listen to him.' Peter, James and John were convinced it was the voice of God.

The disciples did not understand Jesus' reference to rising from the dead although they believed in the resurrection at the end of the world. Being raised to life in the here and now was much harder to grasp and needed some thinking about.

●● **Think and write ...**

1 What does the term Son of Man mean?
2 What did the Jews at the time of Jesus expect of the Messiah?
3 Why were Moses and Elijah present at the Transfiguration?
4 Why was Peter ready to say that Jesus was the Messiah?

●● **Digging deeper**

5 Why do you think Jesus was so stern with Peter?
6 Explain the significance of Moses' and Elijah's presence on the mountain.
7 Why do you think Jesus talked so much about what was going to happen to him?

→ **POSSIBLE APPLICATIONS**

● how people think of Jesus today (page 114)
● Jesus revealed in the world today in the lives of Mother Teresa (page 138), Jackie Pullinger (page 140), Oscar Romero (page 72), Trevor Huddleston (page 34) and Meg Guillebaud (page 146).

Jesus – myth, man or God?

People argued then about who Jesus was. They still argue today. But today the arguments are a little different. Here are some common viewpoints on Jesus that you might hear.

MYTH?

I think Jesus is a MYTH. He never existed.

He is mentioned by early historians such as Josephus, so he must have existed.

If he did exist, he must have been different from the Jesus the Church believes in. What if the stories got exaggerated over the centuries to fit in with what people believed?

The first Christians must have known he was pretty special if they were prepared to die for their belief. Telling stories was the ancient way of remembering history and was usually fairly reliable, and the first stories about him were written down only 40 or so years after he died.

GOOD MAN?

I think Jesus was a prophet. He was a good man who said a lot of wise things and helped people. He set a good example and stood up against injustice and cruelty and condemned religious leaders for hypocrisy. He preached peace, love and FORGIVENESS and looked out for the outcasts.

He made a lot of strange claims for a good man. He said he had power over death and disease, and he forgave people for sin that had nothing to do with him.

There is a lot of symbolism in what Jesus said and did. He had an extraordinary understanding of God.

But he told people that they could be saved through believing in him. If he was just a man, he's dead now and can't save anybody. Surely giving people false hope is not something a good man would do.

I think people today are inspired by the example he set, not by what he said about himself.

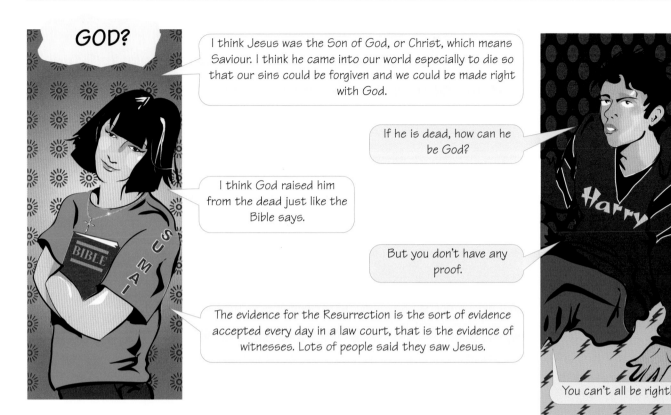

GOD?

I think Jesus was the Son of God, or Christ, which means Saviour. I think he came into our world especially to die so that our sins could be forgiven and we could be made right with God.

If he is dead, how can he be God?

I think God raised him from the dead just like the Bible says.

But you don't have any proof.

The evidence for the Resurrection is the sort of evidence accepted every day in a law court, that is the evidence of witnesses. Lots of people said they saw Jesus.

You can't all be right!

So what now?

If we were to hold **Jason's view** that most of what we know about Jesus is a **myth**, then we would not build our lives on his spiritual teaching although we might follow his moral guidelines. A good many Christians might say there are mythical elements to the Jesus of the Gospels.

If we were to hold **Josie's view** that Jesus was a **good man**, we would be likely to try to live a good life according to his teaching. We might believe that Jesus had great spiritual insight, even though we wouldn't accept that he was God or that he was raised from the dead. We would probably believe that what he taught lives on after his death, and because of his example there is hope for the world. Almost all Christians would say that Jesus was a good man in the fullest sense. Even Muslims would agree.

If we were to hold **Su Mai's view** that Jesus was the **Son of God**, we would make Jesus' teaching central to the way we lived our lives. We would know that we would be forgiven for things we get wrong and we could call on him for help in times of trouble. We would become involved in telling other people about Jesus, and we wouldn't fear death because we would believe Jesus conquered it.

● ● **Discuss**

In groups, discuss the views held by the three characters. Do you think their arguments are convincing? Can you think of other points they might have made?

● ● ● **Activity**

1 Hold a secret ballot in your class to vote for your view. Make a graph to show your class's views on who Jesus was.

● ● **Think and write ...**

2 Essay practice: Do you agree with Harry's comment that they can't all be right? Give your reasons.

18 The parables of Jesus

1 The Sower

Read **Luke 8.4–8, 11–15**.

encounter

●● Think and write: encounter

1 What kinds of people do the different types of ground symbolise?
2 What happened to the seed in each case?

understand

Background

Jesus was talking about the Kingdom of God. This is a kingdom where God's authority and power is accepted. Jesus taught that the Kingdom of God was not a physical kingdom but a spiritual kingdom existing in people's hearts and in heaven.

Membership of this kingdom was not automatic but depended on a person's response to the gospel. This is the context of the parable of the sower.

The meaning of the parable

● The seed symbolised the gospel, the good news about the Kingdom of God.
● The sower is someone who spreads the gospel.
● The places where the seed falls symbolise the different ways in which people respond to the gospel.

The path

People who hear the gospel but reject it straight away. The birds symbolise the devil or whatever prevents people from even thinking about what they have heard.

Among the rocks

People who hear the gospel and for a short while become excited by it, but they do nothing to find out more so eventually the novelty wears off and they stop thinking about it.

The thorns and weeds

People who hear the gospel and for a while accept it and try to live a godly life. But the pressures of everyday life crowd in and they do not have time to develop their spiritual lives seriously.

The good soil

People who hear the gospel and accept it; it becomes the most important thing in their lives. They tell other people about it.

● ● Think and write: understand

3 What does the term 'Kingdom of God' mean?
4 Why are weeds and thorns choking the plant a good symbol of the third type of person who hears the gospel?
5 Why did Jesus tell this parable?
6 Why would it have appealed to his audience?

---

apply 1

A parable for today to explain

The Kingdom of God is like this …

There was once a company, which had invented a kind of toothpaste that prevented tooth decay forever. You only had to use it once a week, not twice a day like the other brands. The No-Nonsense Toothpaste Company advertised it on TV and noted the reactions of four different audiences.

Children saw the advertisement in between cartoons but they weren't interested in toothpaste and switched channels immediately.

People watching a football match saw the advertisement in the break. They thought it was a splendid idea and wouldn't it be just great if it worked. They'd certainly go and buy some. But they quickly forgot about it.

Students saw the advertisement after a late-night movie. They thought the toothpaste would be so cool. They all went out and bought it. But as the weeks and months went by, they forgot they had to clean their teeth once a week with it. There was so much work to do and parties to go to that there simply wasn't time, and eventually they threw the tube away.

Mothers saw the advertisement in the breaks between a popular television soap story in the early evening. 'Once a week brushing and no tooth decay?' they thought. 'Brilliant!' and they rushed out to buy it in bulk. They made sure their entire family used it and told all their friends and relations. Years later they still had no need of the dentist.

● ● ● Activity

7 Choose a modern message such as 'eat a healthy diet', and get it across using a parable. Read your parable to your friends and see whether they get the message.

2 The Good Samaritan

●● **Think and write: encounter**

1 What had happened to the man?

2 What did the Samaritan do to help?

encounter

understand

Read **Luke 10.25–37**.

Background

Jesus told this parable to answer a Jewish lawyer's very practical moral question. It was also to impress on him and other listeners his duty of loving his neighbour as himself, by giving a practical example.

The lawyer knew the answer to the question 'What must I do to inherit eternal life?' but the second part posed a real dilemma: 'Who is my neighbour?'

Were they to treat everyone in the world as their neighbour and love them as they would themselves? Where could they draw the line? Were they to treat outrageous sinners and national enemies as neighbours, or did being bad or an enemy make them cease to qualify as neighbours? Surely neighbours were the people in the same street or those who attended the same synagogue.

Jesus answered the question by telling a very practical story.

Characters in the parable

● The man who was attacked was a **Jew**.
● The man who rescued him was a **Samaritan**. The Jews and the Samaritans fiercely hated each other and, under normal circumstances, the Jew would have rejected the Samaritan's help. Yet the Samaritan had such compassion for the Jew that he overcame all his religious prejudices and hatred, and treated him with extraordinary generosity.
● The **Priest** and the **Levite** did not trouble to help their fellow Jew. They may have considered that they had good reason. To help might have been inconvenient because touching a dead body would have made them ceremonially unclean. They would have had to go through the rituals of purification before being able to enter the Temple and go about their religious duties. Just by looking, they were unable to determine whether the man was dead or alive. They may not have wanted to take the risk. However, Jesus left his listeners in no doubt that these were not valid reasons not to help a dying man.

The meaning of the parable

People love to listen to stories because they can identify what is being taught with a familiar situation. Jesus often used this method to teach about the Kingdom of God and to get across important truths.

Jesus asked the lawyer which of the three men became the neighbour to the man who had been mugged. In other words, Jesus taught that whenever a person comes across someone in need, he should help them as he would like to be helped if he were in desperate need. The issues about who that someone was, whether they were a national enemy or a convicted criminal or a social reject, were irrelevant.

● ● Think and write: understand

3 Why did neither the Priest nor the Levite help the man?
4 Why would Jesus' listeners not expect to hear that a Samaritan helped him?
5 What idea was Jesus trying to get across in this parable?
6 Why did the lawyer need to ask who his neighbour was?
7 Does the parable of the Good Samaritan get Jesus' idea across well? Give your reasons.

● ● ● Activity

9 Act out this parable using contemporary characters.

3 The Lost Son

●● Think and write: encounter

1 Make a flow chart to show the Lost Son's story.
2 Why was the elder brother angry?

Read **Luke 15.11–32** to help you.

understand

Setting

This parable was aimed at the Pharisees. They had been objecting to Jesus associating with tax collectors and other bad characters. Look back at the first part of Luke 15 and read the parable of the lost sheep and the lost coin. The Pharisees would be glad to find both a sheep that was lost and a lost piece of silver, and their friends would understand why they were glad.

Jesus said this earthly joy at finding something that had been lost was like the joy felt in heaven when a person came back to God.

Therefore the father in the story was right to expect his elder son to join in the celebrations when his lost son returned. The elder son thought his father was too soft and that it was grossly unfair on him.

The meaning of the parable – 1

● The elder son symbolised the Pharisees. Through the parable, Jesus told them they were out of sympathy with God and in danger of excluding themselves from the heavenly feast.

● Just as the elder son was indignant with the father for spending time and money on the bad younger brother, so the Pharisees were indignant that Jesus should spend time with sinners. Like the elder brother, they were not glad when these sinners repented.

- Like the elder brother on the farm, the Pharisees had worked hard at keeping the commandments and were proud of their track record, but it never made them feel joyful and they were still unsure whether God really accepted them.
- On the other hand, here were the tax collectors and their like, who had broken pretty well all the commandments and lived disgracefully, being made welcome by Jesus, just by saying sorry. How unfair was that?
- The parable pointed out that in welcoming home the lost son, or sinners, the elder brother, or Pharisees, had not lost out on anything. 'All that I have is yours,' said the father, who of course symbolises God. The elder brother had no feeling of being an heir to all his father had, and in fact talked about having slaved for years for his father. The Pharisees felt the same.

The meaning of the parable – 2

- The second strand to the parable centres around the younger son. The younger son broke all the rules, became degraded in his own eyes and said sorry.
- This is the message of the Gospel that Jesus was explaining in these parables. No matter how bad a person has been, if they repent, God will forgive them and receive them back into his Kingdom. This is called REDEMPTION or salvation. Jesus is sometimes called 'Redeemer', especially in old hymns.

Summary of symbols used in the parable

The father	God
The younger son	sinners
The elder brother	the Pharisees
The farm	the Kingdom of God
The pigs	pigs are unclean to Jews and to work with them symbolised the lowest kind of job
The feast	the heavenly feast to which everyone is invited to share with God at the end of time

● ● Think and write: understand

3 Who do the three characters represent?
4 What is 'redemption'?
5 Why is the younger son described as 'lost'?
6 Explain how the Pharisees were like the elder brother.

● ● Digging deeper

7 'We don't know the true value of something until we've lost it.' Do you agree? Give your reasons.

● ● Discuss

Do you think the elder brother had a justifiable grievance?

● ● ● Activity

8 In groups, illustrate the story showing how both brothers behaved and how the father treated them.

→ POSSIBLE APPLICATIONS

There are many other possible applications for this unit. Each parable contains a number of truths about life and situations that are relevant to contemporary living. You should expect questions on any aspect of the teaching in the parables.

Prejudice and discrimination

DISCRIMINATION happens when one group of people is treated differently from others because of prejudice.

PREJUDICE is a biased opinion against someone or something for no logical reason. It is formed without real knowledge of the person or thing. It often arises from having a fixed mental idea about a group of people. This is called stereotyping and is a major cause of making people feel outcasts from society.

Some common causes of racial/religious prejudice

1 Humans tend to form groups and feel threatened by those not in their group.
2 People coming into this country from abroad come from different cultures and usually speak a different language. This can lead to misunderstandings and the feeling that people of other races are 'inferior'.
3 In times of high unemployment, tensions arise between racial groups because one group fears the other will take its jobs.
4 Racial groups are often used as scapegoats. When something goes wrong in the country, the blame may be unfairly placed on a particular racial group. This happened in Germany in the 1930s and 1940s.
5 The rise in terrorism has made people more afraid of different racial and religious groups. After the Twin Towers were destroyed by terrorists in September 2001, many people became unreasonably suspicious of all Muslims and Asians, even though it was only a small extremist group of people in another country who carried out the attack.

The law about race in Britain

● The Race Relations Act of 1976 made it against the law to discriminate against people on the grounds of race, colour, nationality or ethnic origin. This applied to employment, housing, education, advertising and the provision of goods and services.
● Racial violence is a criminal offence and people can be sent to prison for encouraging or stirring up racial hatred.
● Racial prejudice is not against the law because it is an attitude of mind and therefore cannot be made illegal.

△ Muslim men wait behind a police line at the site of a mass grave near Sipovo in western Bosnia, 2002.

understand

apply 2

Multi-racial Britain

Britain has always been a multi-racial society. Over the centuries, people have migrated to Britain for many reasons.

● The Romans, Vikings and Normans came as **invaders**.

● Others came as **traders** and stayed.

● Many people have come as **refugees** to escape war, famine or religious persecution. For example: Huguenots (French Protestants in the seventeenth century who were persecuted by Catholics in France); Jews at various times over the centuries; and Eastern Europeans to escape ethnic cleansing, which is what happens when a particular group of people is killed because they are not thought to belong to the country in which they live.

● When Britain had an **empire** in the eighteenth and nineteenth centuries, links were made with countries all over the world and many people from those countries came to live in Britain. After the Second World War, Britain was very short of key workers. People from countries such as India, Bangladesh, Pakistan, the West Indies and Far East were invited here to fill **job vacancies**. Since then, many more people have come to Britain as **economic migrants**.

Today, well over three million people in Britain describe themselves as black, Asian or Chinese or say they belong to another non-white group. Nearly half were brought up in Britain and think of themselves as British.

△ The NHS relies on doctors and nurses from many countries.

● ● Think and write …

Practise answering the evaluation questions below, which are examples of those found at the end of each Common Entrance section.

Use the information in this unit to help you form an opinion and be able to support it with examples.

1 What makes people prejudiced against others? Give examples to support your answer.

2 Do you think we have a duty to help people who don't fit into society? Give reasons to support your answer.

3 'Education about other people's beliefs and culture would help to reduce prejudice.' Do you agree? Give reasons for your answer.

● ● Discuss

Is it possible to stamp out prejudice?

● ● ● Activity

4 Divide a page in half vertically. On one side write down the causes of racial and religious prejudice. (You may also add ideas of your own which are not included in this unit.) On the other side give examples. Use newspapers and the internet to help you find examples.

Forgiveness

Northern Ireland has a history of violence, which started because of English intervention in its affairs as long ago as Oliver Cromwell in the seventeenth century. Religious divisions affect every area of life and there has been animosity between CATHOLICS and Protestants ever since.

In November 1987, the IRA blew up the centre of the town of Enniskillen, during the Remembrance Day parade. Eleven people were killed and dozens were injured. The whole world was shocked and outraged by this event. Twenty-year-old nursing student Marie Wilson was killed; her father, Gordon, was injured. Later that day, when Gordon Wilson was released from the hospital, he gave this statement:

△ The aftermath of the bombing in Enniskillen.

'I have no desire for revenge or retaliation. Killing the people who killed my daughter will not bring her back. So I forgive the bombers and I leave everything to God and I believe, someday, I will see my daughter again.'

The whole country was shocked by Gordon's forgiveness. No one had ever forgiven the other side quite so publicly before. For the first time in ages, people began to talk about forgiving one another, forgiving the bombers, and letting go of resentment. This talk of forgiveness and RECONCILIATION contributed to the setting up of the Good Friday peace agreement in 1998. Gordon travelled around the world promoting reconciliation until his death from a heart attack a few years ago.

'I have lost my daughter, and we shall miss her. But I bear no ill will. I bear no grudge,' he told the BBC. 'Dirty sort of talk is not going to bring her back to life.' He said he forgave her killers and added: 'I shall pray for those people tonight and every night.'

△ Enniskillen today.

◁ Gordon Wilson.

Father John Dear is an American Catholic Priest who, while he was living in Northern Ireland, decided to go to Enniskillen and meet Gordon Wilson's widow, Joan. He writes this about their meeting:

She invited me in for a cup of tea that afternoon and I asked her, 'Joan, how did he do it? How did you and Gordon forgive the people who killed your daughter?' This is what she said to me. 'Gordon and I had been married for thirty years, and every night before we went to bed, we knelt down together and prayed the Lord's prayer. Every night for thirty years! When Gordon was in the hospital that afternoon, he said to me, "We have to forgive. Otherwise, we can never pray the Lord's prayer again." We wanted to be able to say to God, "Forgive us our trespasses, as we forgive those who trespass against us." So we forgave the murderers, and we were able to continue praying the Lord's prayer.'

From www.fatherjohndear.org.

●●● Activity

1 Imagine you witnessed the attack. Write about what happened and your thoughts when you heard Gordon Wilson forgiving the killers.

●● Think and write ...

2 'I shall pray for those people tonight and every night.' About whom was Gordon Wilson talking?
3 Gordon Wilson said he could not pray the Lord's Prayer again unless he forgave his daughter's killers. Look up the Lord's Prayer and highlight the section to which he was referring.
4 In what ways did the people in Enniskillen react to Gordon Wilson's words?

●● Digging deeper

5 What do we learn about forgiveness from what happened?
6 Forgiveness is the beginning of freedom. Do you agree? Give reasons for your answer.

19 The sentence, crucifixion and burial of Jesus

Why did Jesus die?

●● Starter

Discuss: Why is this story so well known?

A [11]But the chief priests stirred up the crowd to have Pilate release Barabbas instead.

[12] 'What shall I do, then, with the one you call the king of the Jews?' Pilate asked them.

[13] 'Crucify him!' they shouted.

[14] 'Why? What crime has he committed?' asked Pilate.

But they shouted all the louder, 'Crucify him!'

[15]Wanting to satisfy the crowd, Pilate released Barabbas to them. He had Jesus flogged, and handed him over to be crucified.

[16]The soldiers led Jesus away into the palace (that is, the Praetorium) and called together the whole company of soldiers. [17]They put a purple robe on him, then twisted together a crown of thorns and set it on him. [18]And they began to call out to him, 'Hail, king of the Jews!' [19]Again and again they struck him on the head with a staff and spat on him. Falling on their knees, they paid homage to him. [20]And when they had mocked him, they took off the purple robe and put his own clothes on him. Then they led him out to crucify him.

[21]A certain man from Cyrene, Simon, the father of Alexander and Rufus, was passing by on his way in from the country, and they forced him to carry the cross. [22]They brought Jesus to the place called Golgotha (which means The Place of the Skull). [23]Then they offered him wine mixed with myrrh, but he did not take it. [24]And they crucified him. Dividing up his clothes, they cast lots to see what each would get.

[25]It was the third hour when they crucified him. [26]The written notice of the charge against him read: the king of the Jews. [23]They crucified two robbers with him, one on his right and one on his left.

[29]Those who passed by hurled insults at him, shaking their heads and saying, 'So! You who are going to destroy the temple and build it in three days, [30]come down and save yourself!'

[31]In the same way the chief priests and the teachers of the law mocked him among themselves. 'He saved others,' they said, 'but he can't save himself! [32]Let this Christ, this King of Israel, come down now from the cross, that we may see and believe.' Those crucified with him also heaped insults on him.

[33]At the sixth hour, darkness came over the whole land until the ninth hour. [34]And at the ninth hour Jesus cried out in a loud voice, 'Eloi, Eloi, lama sabachthani?' – which means, 'My God, my God, why have you forsaken me?'.

[35]When some of those listening near heard this, they said, 'Listen, he's calling Elijah.'

[36]One man ran, filled a sponge with wine vinegar, put it on a stick, and offered it to Jesus to drink. 'Now leave him alone. Let's see if Elijah comes to take him down,' he said.

[37]With a loud cry, Jesus breathed his last.

³⁸The curtain of the temple was torn in two from top to bottom. ³⁹And when the centurion, who stood there in front of Jesus, heard his cry and saw how he died, he said, 'Surely this man was the Son of God!'

⁴⁶So Joseph bought some linen cloth, took down the body, wrapped it in the linen, and placed it in a tomb cut out of rock. Then he rolled a stone against the entrance of the tomb.

Mark 15.11–39, 46.

B

● ● ● **Activity**

Read the full text from the Bible in **Mark 15.6–47**. Make a list of the most important things in the story and present them in picture form or as a chart or concept map.

△ Ian Bruce painted this picture while a boy at Eton. What does it tell you about how he understands our part in the crucifixion?

a) Why do many people wear crosses and crucifixes?

b) Study the crosses. What different messages do they convey?

The sentence, crucifixion and burial of Jesus

The Jewish religious leaders wanted Jesus dead because:

1 He was too popular. Everywhere he went, he attracted people and even now, an enormous crowd had turned out to welcome Jesus into Jerusalem for the Passover festival.
2 He threatened their authority and was outspoken in his condemnation of them.
3 He made himself equal to God, which to them was blasphemy.

They had no authority to have him executed and a religious reason would not be enough to convince the Romans he should die. Under Roman law the charges were as follows:

1 He was leading the Jewish nation's loyalty away from Rome.
2 He had forbidden taxes to be paid to Rome – the usual accusation against Zealots.
3 Jesus had claimed the title 'king', which was a treasonable offence.

The events

● Jesus was scourged, which involved being whipped with a leather thong studded with metal and bone.
● Soldiers made a mockery of the charge against him – that he was a king.
● The routine of crucifixion was that the criminal had to carry his own cross. He walked with four soldiers and one went ahead of them carrying a board on which was written the prisoner's crime. This was later fixed to the cross. They took the longest route possible so that everyone had the chance to see and be warned.
● Jesus was too weak to carry his own cross so a man called Simon of Cyrene was made to carry it for him. Simon's son Rufus became an eminent figure in the church and was a close friend of St Paul.
● A group of women always went to crucifixions to offer some pain relief, but Jesus refused it.
● Everyone insulted and mocked him. They challenged him by saying they would believe his claims if he came down from the cross. Look back to the Devil's temptation in Unit 13.
● Jesus' words from Psalm 22 are in Aramaic so that the confusion with Elijah makes sense. Christians believe that in that moment, Jesus was taking on himself the punishment for the sins of the human race. This separated him from God and so caused his anguish.

- Two significant things happened at the moment of Jesus' death:
  a) The curtain dividing the Holy of Holies from the rest of the Temple was ripped in two. God was believed to be present in a very special way in the Holy of Holies and so Christians see this as a symbol of Jesus' death removing the barrier between God and humans.
  b) A hard-bitten soldier who was a complete stranger to Jesus made a tribute to him by saying that he must have been the Son of God. He probably meant that Jesus had been a very great man, even godlike.
- Jesus died at 3 o'clock on Friday afternoon and as the Sabbath began at 6 o'clock, there were only three hours left to take him down from the cross and bury him.

What does Jesus' death mean to Christians today?

They believe that:

- Jesus gave his life as a **sacrifice** for human sin. The Old Testament helps explain this because in the ritual of sacrifice, God accepted the life of the animal as an atonement for the sins of the people. Atonement means getting back into a right relationship with God – 'at-one-ment'. It means being forgiven by him. These sacrifices had to be offered every year. Jesus' sacrifice was once and for all.
- Jesus' death **removed the barrier of sin**, allowing humans direct access to God.

●● Think and write . . .

1 Why did the Jewish religious leaders want Jesus dead?
2 Why did the bystanders taunt him when he was on the cross?
3 What is the significance of what happened at the moment of his death?

●● Digging deeper

4 Why might it be appropriate that Jesus died with two sinners?
5 How might Jesus' death be seen as a sacrifice?
6 Why did Jesus die?

→ **POSSIBLE APPLICATIONS**

- self-sacrifice (page 130)
- someone in recent history who has been prepared to suffer for his/her beliefs (page 28)
- Oscar Romero (page 72).
- capital punishment (page 46).

Miracle on the River Kwai

There are many wartime stories about self-sacrifice. This one concerns a soldier of the Argyll and Sutherland Highlanders, who was taken prisoner of war by the Japanese. He was forced to work on the notorious Burma Railway, building a bridge over the River Kwai (see pictures B and C).

A The day's work had ended; the tools were being counted, as usual. As the party was about to be dismissed, the guard shouted that a shovel was missing. He insisted that someone had stolen it to sell to the Thais. Striding up and down before the men, he ranted and denounced them for their wickedness, and most unforgivable of all, their ingratitude to the Emperor. As he raved, he worked himself up into a paranoid fury. Screaming in broken English, he demanded that the guilty one step forward to take his punishment. No one moved; the guard's rage reached new heights of violence.

'All die! All die!' he shrieked.

To show that he meant what he said, he cocked his rifle, put it to his shoulder and looked down the sights, ready to fire at the first man at the end of them.

At that moment the Argyll stepped forward, stood stiffly to attention, and said calmly, 'I did it'.

The guard unleashed all his whipped-up hate; he kicked the helpless prisoner and beat him with his fists. Still the Argyll stood rigidly to attention, with the blood streaming down his face. His silence goaded the guard to an excess of rage. Seizing his rifle by the barrel, he lifted it high over his head and, with a final howl, brought it down on the skull of the Argyll, who sank limply to the ground and did not move. Although it was perfectly clear that he was dead, the guard continued to beat him and stopped only when exhausted.

The men of the work detail picked up their comrade's body, shouldered their tools and marched back to camp. When the tools were counted again at the guard-house no shovel was missing.

From *Miracle on the River Kwai* by Ernest Gordon.

●● Discuss

What kind of thing might prompt you to give your life to save another person?

●●● Activity

1 Read story A. Imagine you are the prisoner at whom the guard was pointing when the soldier stood forward. Write a letter home to your family describing what happened and how you felt.

understand

apply

◁ Prisoners of war were used as labourers to build the railway through Burma.

◁ A forced march along the railway, from the film of Ernest Gordon's book.

●● Digging deeper

6 Do you think the Argyll soldier made the right decision?

7 Would you have tried to stop him? Give your reasons.

8 It is often said that war brings out the best in people. Do you agree? Give your reasons.

●● Think and write ...

2 In story A, why did the Argyll soldier say that he had taken the shovel?

3 If you were one of the other prisoners, how would you have felt when the shovel was rediscovered?

4 In what way is the reason for Jesus' death similar to the reason for the Argyll soldier's?

5 In what way is it different?

encounter

●● **Starter**

Discuss:
1 Do you believe Jesus came back from the dead?
2 What other explanations could there be for the empty tomb?
3 Do you always have to see something in order to believe it?

A ¹Early on the first day of the week, while it was still dark, Mary Magdalene went to the tomb and saw that the stone had been removed from the entrance. ²So she came running to Simon Peter and the other disciple, the one Jesus loved, and said, 'They have taken the Lord out of the tomb, and we don't know where they have put him!'

³So Peter and the other disciple started for the tomb. ⁴Both were running, but the other disciple outran Peter and reached the tomb first. ⁵He bent over and looked in at the strips of linen lying there but did not go in. ⁶Then Simon Peter, who was behind him, arrived and went into the tomb. He saw the strips of linen lying there, ⁷as well as the cloth that had been around Jesus' head. The cloth was folded up by itself, separate from the linen. ⁸Finally the other disciple, who had reached the tomb first, also went inside. He saw and believed. ⁹(They still did not understand from Scripture that Jesus had to rise from the dead.) ¹⁰Then the disciples went back to their homes.

John 20.1–10.

B ¹¹But Mary stood outside the tomb crying. As she wept, she bent over to look into the tomb ¹²and saw two angels in white, seated where Jesus' body had been, one at the head and the other at the foot.

¹³They asked her, 'Woman, why are you crying?'

'They have taken my Lord away,' she said, 'and I don't know where they have put him.' ¹⁴At this, she turned round and saw Jesus standing there, but she did not realise that it was Jesus.

¹⁵'Woman,' he said, 'why are you crying? Who is it you are looking for?'

Thinking he was the gardener, she said, 'Sir, if you have carried him away, tell me where you have put him, and I will get him.'

¹⁶Jesus said to her, 'Mary.'

She turned towards him and cried out in Aramaic, 'Rabboni!' (which means Teacher).

¹⁷Jesus said, 'Do not hold on to me, for I have not yet returned to the Father. Go instead to my brothers and tell them, "I am returning to my Father and your Father, to my God and your God."'

¹⁸Mary Magdalene went to the disciples with the news: 'I have seen the Lord!' And she told them that he had said these things to her.

John 20.11–18.

C ¹⁹On the evening of that first day of the week, when the disciples were together, with the doors locked for fear of the Jews, Jesus came and stood among them and said, 'Peace be with you!' ²⁰After he said this, he showed them his hands and side. The disciples were overjoyed when they saw the Lord.

²¹Again Jesus said, 'Peace be with you! As the Father has sent me, I am sending you.' ²²And with that he breathed on them and said, 'Receive the Holy Spirit. ²³If you forgive anyone his sins, they are forgiven; if you do not forgive them, they are not forgiven.'

²⁴Now Thomas (called Didymus), one of the Twelve, was not with the disciples when Jesus came. ²⁵So the other disciples told him, 'We have seen the Lord!'

But he said to them, 'Unless I see the nail marks in his hands and put my finger where the nails were, and put my hand into his side, I will not believe it.'

²⁶A week later his disciples were in the house again, and Thomas was with them. Though the doors were locked, Jesus came and stood among them and said, 'Peace be with you!' ²⁷Then he said to Thomas, 'Put your finger here; see my hands. Reach out your hand and put it into my side. Stop doubting and believe.'

²⁸Thomas said to him, 'My Lord and my God!'

²⁹Then Jesus told him, 'Because you have seen me, you have believed; blessed are those who have not seen and yet have believed.'

John 20.19–29.

●● Discuss

The artist (above) has changed one significant detail from the written version in source C. Can you spot it?

●●● Activity

In groups, present one of these stories in any way you like. It could be as art, poetry or drama.

The Resurrection

△ *He is Risen* by He Qi. What moment in the story does this picture show? Who are the characters and what are they holding?

This account shows how the disciples were convinced that Jesus had risen from the dead.

The garden tomb

John and **Peter** were convinced by the absence of Jesus' body and by the position of the grave clothes, which looked as though they had not been disturbed.

Mary Magdalene was convinced by a man she met in the garden. Jesus must have looked different or she would have recognised him. She did not understand that Jesus was no longer tied to earthly life so he had to tell her he had not yet gone up to God and she must not try to hold on to his physical presence.

Jesus gave her an important message: he was returning to his father and his God, who was also the disciples' spiritual father and their God.

The significance of Jesus appearing to Mary Magdalene is threefold:

1 She had led a sinful life, had repented and followed Jesus. Jesus' appearance to her would reinforce his acceptance of her into his Kingdom.
2 She was a woman. Under Jewish law they had no rights. Jesus showed that he treated all people equally.
3 Christians are reminded that Jesus came to save outcasts and sinners. This is the hope of salvation.

Jesus appears to his disciples

The disciples were hiding from the Jewish authorities when Jesus suddenly appeared. He said 'Peace be with you' twice, to reassure them. Then he breathed his Holy Spirit on them, as the holy wind would blow the Spirit on them on the day of Pentecost (Acts 2). This Holy Spirit is the enabling power of God. The disciples would now have the courage and ability to spread the gospel.

Jesus also gave them the authority to forgive sins. That is why priests give the absolution after the congregation or an individual has confessed their sins. Absolution means forgiveness.

This is an extraordinary story and people have tried to rationalise it by talking of mass hallucinations. The early Christians firmly believed in a bodily resurrection and John included the account of Jesus showing the holes in his hands and in his side. The report of blood and water pouring from his side when on the cross is consistent with what would happen if a spear were thrust into the heart after death had occurred. The Gospel presents this as evidence that Jesus had really died and then risen again.

However, although Jesus appeared in physical form, he was not like other people because he was now able to appear and disappear at will. The disciples who saw Jesus accepted that he had risen. Thomas, who was not there, did not believe the others at first. Jesus commended those who had not seen him and yet would believe. He was referring to future believers. Thomas' statement of faith, 'My Lord and my God!' demonstrated the shift in the disciples' thinking to accepting that the risen Jesus was God.

The evidence for the Resurrection

The Christian faith is centred round the belief that Jesus rose from the dead, so let us examine what evidence there is.

1 The disciples were turned from a frightened group, who had just seen their leader crucified, into a strong courageous band who told everyone that Jesus was alive. They were prepared to preach the Resurrection and to die for that belief. This sudden transformation is undisputed.
2 The early Church put belief in the Resurrection into their creed.
3 St Paul, one of the Apostles and early missionaries, did a study of the evidence. He said that Jesus had appeared to five hundred people at the same time as well as individually to the disciples and some women. Most would have still been alive and it is reasonable to assume that some had spoken to Paul. Jesus had also appeared in a special way to Paul.
4 The Gospels all contain stories of Jesus appearing to his disciples, both collectively and individually.
5 The Gospels all include evidence of an empty grave. If there had been a body, the Romans and the Jewish religious leaders would surely have found it as it was in their interests to put an end to the rumours that Jesus was alive.
6 The stories are written simply and do not contain any symbolism that needs special decoding or understanding.

Another way of understanding the Resurrection

Some Christians say that the important thing about the Resurrection is not the physical body, but the spiritual one. They say it does not matter whether the tomb was empty or not, or whether Jesus had an earthly form when he spoke to the disciples and to Mary. What is important is that Jesus was and is really present in people's lives and can help them to live a holy life.

●● **Discuss**

Does it make a difference to the Christian faith whether Jesus' Resurrection was physical or spiritual?

●● **Think and write ...**

1 What convinced Peter and John that Jesus was risen?
2 What did Jesus mean when he told Mary not to hold on to him?
3 Why did he tell Thomas to touch his hands and side?

●● **Digging deeper**

4 Write down what you think are the three most compelling pieces of evidence for the Resurrection. Write the reasons for your choice.
5 What was the significance of Jesus' breathing on the disciples?

→ **POSSIBLE APPLICATIONS**

● attitudes to death (page 136)
● evidence for an afterlife (page 137).

Death: an end or a beginning?

▷ Pope John Paul II's funeral, 2005.

On 8 April 2005, Pope John Paul II was buried. Millions of people went to Rome in order to mourn him. For some it was a time to grieve for their spiritual leader; for others it was a moment of great national and historical pride; and for all of them it was a time to pay tribute to a great man. His funeral expressed more than sorrow at his death, however, it expressed the joyful hope shared by Christians throughout the world that he was now with God. In his sermon, Cardinal Ratzinger, who became the next Pope, said, 'We can be sure that our beloved Pope is standing at the window of the Father's house, that he sees us and he blesses us.'

Historical attitudes to death

Before modern medicine, deaths in the family were common, especially among children. This exposure to death meant that people talked about it naturally and were generally less afraid of it than they are now. Funerals, like baptisms and weddings, were rites of passage and a part of everyday life.

Today, we prefer to hide death away in hospitals and old people's homes. We pretend it doesn't happen and spend our time trying to stay young. It has become as taboo a subject as sex was in Victorian England.

At some point in our history, human beings began to think about what happens to a person when they die. It is difficult to imagine non-existence, and even very primitive people believed in a god or gods. The Neanderthals buried their dead in the foetal position, perhaps symbolising rebirth. Today most religions believe in an afterlife. Muslims believe in Paradise. Hindus believe in the reincarnation of living beings in a sort of hierarchy of existence; the way a person lives dictating what they will be reborn as. Buddhists have a similar belief but for them rebirth is a sign of imperfection. Only when they cease to exist will they have attained what they call 'Enlightenment'.

Christians believe that there is life after death. They believe that people keep their individuality and identity but have spiritual bodies. Christian funeral services stress the belief that the person who has died will be raised to spiritual life with Jesus in heaven.

△ A funeral service in Angola. What do you notice about this funeral?

Hymns are sung to remind those grieving that death is not the end. Because of this faith, Christian funerals are often times of rejoicing that a person has gone to be with God.

Does what we believe about death influence the way we live our lives?

A famous eighteenth-century French philosopher called Blaise Pascal thought that it probably should. He said that if a person who believed in life after death were wrong, he would never know about it. But if a person who believed there is no life after death were wrong, the consequences could be very serious! This is known as Pascal's Wager.

The Archbishop of Canterbury made this comment in his 2004 Easter Sermon:

'... the goodness of the Resurrection news is most evident for those who have lost people they love to any sort of incomprehensible evil – the tragedies of dementia, the apparent meaninglessness of accident, the horrors of violence or injustice.'

● ● **Think and write ...**

1 Why is death a taboo subject in today's society?
2 How would you comfort someone who was bereaved?

● ● **Digging deeper**

3 'Without the hope of life after death, life would be meaningless.' Do you agree? Give your reasons.

● ● **Discuss**

Does belief in life after death make losing a loved one easier?

Mother Teresa: serving the poor in Calcutta

△ Mother Teresa.

B

We may wonder
whom can I love and serve?
Where is the face of God
to whom I can pray?
The answer is simple.
That naked one.
That lonely one.
That unwanted one
is my brother and my sister.
If we have no peace,
it is because
we have forgotten
that we belong to each other.

'Where is the face of God?', Mother Teresa.

Who else in this world reaches out to the friendless and
the needy so naturally, so simply, so effectively?
She lives the truth that prayer is devotion, prayer is
service. Service is her concern, her religion, her redemption.
To meet her is to feel utterly humble, to sense the power of
tenderness, the strength of love.

Indira Gandhi, Prime Minister of India, 1966–1977
and 1980–1984.

Her call from God

Mother Teresa always wanted to be a nun and joined the Sisters of Loreto
in Dublin. However, she felt God calling her to work in India so she
travelled to Darjeeling where she took her vows of poverty, chastity,
obedience and charity in 1931. She chose the name Sister Teresa. After
that she went to work in a convent school in Calcutta (now known as
Kolkata) where her room overlooked the poorest slums of the Moti Jheel
area. She was shocked by what she saw and began taking basic
medicine to the poor. Gradually she realised where her future lay: 'I
realised I had the call … to be God's love in action to the poorest of the
poor'.

● ● **Discuss**

If she had sought the
limelight, would Mother
Teresa's work have
been as effective?

Her work in Calcutta

The Pope gave permission for Sister Teresa to start a new order of nuns and so the Missionaries of Charity began. She started several projects to help those worst off in society. She said, 'Prayer without action is no prayer at all.'

△ Look at the poster in the top right of the picture. How did Mother Teresa's work put this aim into practice?

● She set up a special town for lepers with its own church and school.

● She started schools for the poor. She had no money for food but said that God always provided for her.

● She opened a home for the destitute dying. These were people who were dying in the streets and had no one to care for them. The home was in Khalighat and backed onto the Kali Temple. Kali is the Hindu goddess of destruction. At first there was a great deal of suspicion and opposition. People threw stones at her and her nuns, accusing them of converting the poor to Christianity. Then one day Mother Teresa saw a crowd of people on the pavement and in the middle lay a man dying in a pool of mess. No one would touch him because he had cholera, a much-feared disease. Mother Teresa picked him up and took him into the home where she nursed and cared for him. When he eventually died, surrounded by people who cared, he was happy. It turned out that the man was a priest from the Kali Temple. After that there was no more trouble.

● She named the home 'Nirmal Hriday', which means 'The Place of the Pure Heart'. It was her work here for which she is best remembered, although as one of her nuns said of her, 'the remarkable thing about Mother Teresa was that she was ordinary'. The home radiated peace and no one was turned away. More than 42,000 people have been taken there over the years.

● There are now centres of the Missionaries of Charity all over the world caring for the poor and outcast from society, including Shishu Bhavan, a home for abandoned children.

Mother Teresa's tireless efforts on behalf of world peace brought her a number of important humanitarian awards, including the Nobel Peace Prize in 1979. She said such earthly rewards were important only if they helped her help the world's needy.

●● **Think and write . . .**

1 What did she do for the people of Calcutta?
2 Why was there opposition to Nirmal Hriday?
3 Why did this opposition end?

●● **Digging deeper**

4 What did Mother Teresa mean by the phrase, 'God's love in action'?
5 What does her poem 'Where is the face of God?' mean?

Jackie's dream

From the time she was at school, Jackie Pullinger felt God was calling her to be a missionary and, while she was a student at the Royal College of Music, she felt the urge to go to Hong Kong in particular.

Setting sail for Hong Kong

Jackie was only 22 and no missionary society would take her because she was too young. However, the vicar of her church said that if she believed God wanted her to work in Hong Kong, she should go.

She put together all her money, and bought a one-way ticket by boat. When she arrived, she got a job teaching music in a primary school. This school was inside a place called the Walled City, which was ruled by gangs of youths called Triads and was the most dangerous place on the island. Everyone was poor in the Walled City and many were on drugs.

△ Jackie Pullinger with Lee Fai, a homeless man whom she helped in Hong Kong.

Working in the Walled City

She started a youth club and at first the young men and boys who made up the gangs laughed at her and assumed she was rich and would soon go home to the West. When she didn't, and they realised she had no money, they began to take her seriously. People wondered that a woman could do this work. Jackie replied:

'If God had sent a man they'd have beaten him up. Men are threatening to men, but women, especially in Chinese culture, are treated with disregard ... So you see, it's wonderful he sent me. They could disregard me because I was not a threat to their maleness and all that made them gangsters.'

Gradually she gained the trust of the young men, and they began to see that she really cared about them. When they wanted to come off drugs, they were able to do so with less pain because Jackie prayed with them.

△ The Walled City, Hong Kong.

Jackie challenges Goko, the Triad gang's leader

(Poon Sui Jeh is Jackie's Chinese name.)

Goko: Poon Sui Jeh, you have a power that I don't have. If my brothers get hooked on drugs I have them beaten up . . . but I can't make them quit. But I've watched you. And I believe Jesus can. So I'm going to send all my addicts to you.

Jackie: What you really mean, Goko, is that you want me to help your boys get off drugs so that you can have them back again to work for you. Triads never give up one of their members. Once you become a Triad, you remain one for life. Christians can't serve two bosses; they have to follow either Christ or you. So my answer is no.

Goko: OK. If there is anyone who wants to follow your Jesus, I give up my right to them. You can have all my rotten brothers.

Jackie: That's fine by me; Jesus came for the rotten ones anyhow.

Adapted from *Chasing the Dragon* by Jackie Pullinger.
Chasing the dragon means smoking opium.

△ The symbol of the Triads.

Although Jackie never asked for money, people sent it and she was able to open houses like St Stephen's, where drug addicts can go to get off drugs.

Of course, not all addicts became reformed characters overnight, and there were many setbacks. In a recent conference she said that when you are dealing with the poor, you go on giving, even when they steal from you, when they go back on drugs after all your efforts. It is then that you find God's grace.

The Walled City was torn down in 1991 but Jackie's work among the poor and drug addicts goes on.

● ● Discuss

a) Is it necessary to go abroad to help the poor?

b) Can foreigners like Jackie achieve more than native Christians?

● ● Think and write . . .

1 Describe how Jackie came to be in Hong Kong.

2 Where did she work when she arrived?

3 What are the Triads?

4 Why was Jackie in a good position to help them?

5 What opportunity did Goko give her?

● ● ● Activity

Look at photo A. Find out how Jackie helped Lee Fai. Your teacher can give you a sheet to help you.

● ● Digging deeper

6 'Jesus came for the rotten ones anyhow.' What did Jackie mean by this?

7 Why did she refuse to compromise with Goko?

8 'You go on giving . . .' Explain what Jackie meant by this description of working with the poor.

23 Dame Cicely Saunders and the hospice movement

△ 'You matter because you are you and you matter until the moment you die.' (Cicely Saunders)

Cicely Saunders was a nurse, a social worker and then a doctor. She devoted her life to the care of the terminally ill.

How did it all start?

While working at St Thomas' Hospital in London, she met a Polish Jew called David Tasma who had terminal cancer. He was only 40. She followed up his case and visited him 25 times in the two months he took to die. He spoke of how much her visits had meant to him and left her £500 in his will. She decided to use this money to help terminally ill people. Along with other professionals, she realised the importance of supporting people through the end stages of an illness. There was a need to prepare patients for their deaths and support bereaved families.

Her vision for a hospice

She retrained as a doctor and became a pioneer in palliative care – treating the symptoms of an incurable illness. The first HOSPICE, St Christopher's, was opened in 1967 in London. She said its aim was 'to recognise and treat both the needs of the patient as a whole person and the needs of the family, to alleviate suffering rather than fight the disease, and to see dying as a time where there is still the potential for healing and growth.' She became medical director, then chairman of the hospice. She was made a Dame in 1980 and died in 2005.

There are now hospices like St Christopher's all over the world.

△ A patient and nurse at St Christopher's.

Saunders and the euthanasia debate

EUTHANASIA has come to mean 'the act of bringing about an easy death', sometimes called 'mercy killing'. It is still illegal in Britain although it is an ongoing debate. Cicely Saunders was against euthanasia because she saw it as the failure of someone or of society to give the dying person the care they needed.

She believed euthanasia was **wrong** for the following reasons:

● Old people might feel pressure to end their lives so as not to be a burden on their families. One elderly woman said, 'human nature being what it is, euthanasia wouldn't remain voluntary for very long'.
● There are powerful drugs available that make a dignified death possible. People do not need to be afraid of a painful death. Doctors do not have to start a series of heroic treatments when a patient is near death. Their commitment is to provide appropriate treatment.
● Hospices provide a caring environment where terminally ill people can die with dignity and without pain, so there is no need for euthanasia. She wrote, 'If care gives a sense of personal worth to the end, living through this part of life brings reconciliation and achievements, and families live on afterwards without the crippling questions and regrets that ... I feel would follow euthanasia.'

◐ ● Think and write ...

1 Why did Cicely Saunders begin the hospice movement?
2 What were the aims of the hospice?
3 Explain why Cicely Saunders was against euthanasia.

◐ ● Digging deeper

4 Explain how the hospice movement has brought comfort to the dying.
5 'No one has the right to take life.' In the context of the terminally ill, do you agree with this statement? Give your reasons.

There are other powerful arguments **against** euthanasia:

It would be the slippery slope to a situation where other people could also make the decision about whether someone lives or dies.

Many people say that because life comes from God, only God has the right to end it. It also goes against the commandment 'do not kill'.

Arguments against euthanasia

A patient might not be able to make a rational decision, or might change their mind but be unable to tell the doctor.

Some people get better.

There are of course, strong arguments **in favour** of people having the right to decide when they die:

Someone on a life-support machine, or terminally ill, could die when they choose.

Suicide is legal, so why not allow people who wish to die to have help doing so?

They could die with their families around them in a loving atmosphere.

Arguments for euthanasia

It would take away from the fear of a painful and undignified death.

People would be spared the agony of watching someone they love die a slow and painful death.

Animals are not made to suffer: the same compassion should be extended to humans.

Helen House, a hospice for children

Website: www.helenanddouglas.org.uk

▷ Helen House, near Oxford.

What is Helen House?

Families who have a very sick child usually want to look after their child at home if they possibly can. Knowing that your child is going to die puts an enormous strain on the whole family and it can be an exhausting and lonely process.

Helen House is a **hospice** where children, from birth to 18, with life-shortening conditions can spend a few days or weeks being looked after. (Life-shortening means they are unlikely to live far into adulthood.) It is a place where they and their families can stay and find practical and emotional support. The mother of one child, for example, had not had an unbroken night's sleep for fourteen years until she came to Helen House. Many children are able to have fun there too. This support for the whole family continues through the child's illness and death, and beyond.

Helen House was built in the grounds of an Anglican convent and founded by an Anglican nun called Sister Frances Dominica. Although the foundation is a Christian one and there is a visiting chaplain, families of other faiths or no faith can receive spiritual support and pastoral care through the hospice's links with local faith communities.

Douglas House, in the same grounds, looks after young people aged 16–35. Helen and Douglas House are run as a charity and funded almost entirely by donations. They have about 300 young people on their books, with illnesses such as muscular dystrophy, cancer and Batten's, which is a degenerative brain disease.

Three types of care are offered:

● **Respite**, where young people with or without their families can have a rest from their normal routine at home.
● **Palliative**, where distressing symptoms are treated. Young people's mental and emotional needs are looked after too.
● **End of life**, where young people are cared for as they die.

How is the Helen House hospice different from a hospital?

- Hospitals tend to look for cures to make you better. A hospice provides care where there is no hope of getting better, but it is not about dying; it's about 'adding life to years'.
- It offers one nurse or carer to one child.
- It is like a home. For example the whole family can stay and meals can be eaten together.
- Children can go on trips such as to the cinema or shopping. Sometimes special trips are arranged, such as going in a helicopter.
- There is a games and computer room, a music room, an art room, a spa room with jacuzzi, and a multi-sensory room where the walls and floors are padded and it has special lights. Such a room can particularly help children who have impaired senses, for example, if they are blind they can enjoy feeling the different materials.
- Every room has the latest equipment such as television and DVDs.

●● Think and write ...

1 What is Helen House?
2 In what ways does it help families of sick children?
3 How is it different from a hospital?
4 What activities can children do at Helen House?

<u>A 12-year-old's day at Helen House</u>

8.00	I get up.
8.30	I have my medicine and my breakfast. I can have breakfast in bed if I like.
9.00	I have a bath or a shower.
10.00	I have some physiotherapy in the spa.
10.30	I have some lessons with a teacher. I can choose what I do. I like music therapy and making things in the hobbies room.
12.30	We all have lunch in the dining room.
1.30	I have a rest
2.30	I go for a walk with the person looking after me if it is a sunny day.
3.30	Sometimes I have an aromatherapy massage which is really nice.
4.15	I watch a DVD.
6.00	We all have supper. The food is delicious.
7.15	The younger children go to bed, but I can play on the computers for a while.

△ A family visiting Helen House

What children say about Helen House

It's my favourite holiday camp.

It feels like a big family.

It's like a hotel.

I love Helen House because it's a very happy place and it makes me happy too.

●● Digging deeper

5 The children all say positive things about Helen House (see left). Why do you think that is?
6 What kind of support might the family of a sick child need?
7 Draw a chart to show how a typical day in Helen House is different from and the same as a typical day in your life.
8 What would you say is the guiding principle of Helen House?

There are two main ethnic groups in Rwanda: the Hutu and the Tutsi. The Hutu hate the Tutsi and in 1994 they rampaged through the country murdering all the Tutsi they could find – men, women and children. Children as young as ten were forced into the army and made to kill people they knew. Somewhere between 800,000 and 1 million people were killed, most of them Tutsis. Three million fled the country.

◁ Skulls at Ntamara Church in Kigali, one of the many churches that were the scene of massacres during the genocide. This woman lost her five children during the atrocities.

Meg Guillebaud's work bringing unity and reconciliation

Meg Guillebaud was brought up in Rwanda where her parents were missionaries. In 1976 she trained in Britain for the priesthood and was one of the first women to be ordained as a deacon.

In 1995 Meg returned to Rwanda, initially for four months, but very soon realised that God wanted her to work there permanently. She listened to the horror stories her friends had to tell. Everyone had lost someone they loved but they still believed that somehow God would bring hope out of the disaster.

The Bishop of Byumba, in the north of Rwanda, said the priority was to teach the Gospel: 'Material needs will help but unless we change the hearts of the people there is no use in helping them physically.'

Rebuilding lives

There are about 30,000 widows and orphans in Rwanda. Meg and her mother Elisabeth set up schemes to help those from both Tutsi and Hutu communities rebuild their lives.

- Sewing groups taught skills that would generate a small income.
- Listening to the stories others had to tell helped people to come to terms with what had happened, and started the process of forgiving those who had wronged them.

△ Meg Guillebaud.

● Training Church leaders from both ethnic groups, who would go back to their villages and help bring about RECONCILIATION within their own congregations.
● Visiting people who were ill and dying.

In March 2004 Meg received an MBE from the Queen, for her 'services with regard to unity and reconciliation in Rwanda'

Gacaca courts

Many of the killers are now being released back into local communities. There are so many of them that they cannot all be tried in national courts.

Village courts, called Gacaca courts (pronounced *gashasha*), are being set up and prisoners are being sent back to the villages where they committed their crimes to be tried by the village elders, the Inyangamugayo, who will decide their punishment.

The guilty are expected to do three things:

1 Tell the truth about what they have done.
2 Ask forgiveness from their victims' families.
3 Make up for what they have done, either by punishment or by payment of some kind.

By following this course of action, reconciliation can become a reality.

The scarf

One of the ways Meg Guillebaud teaches Christians to forgive is through a little drama sketch devised by Rhiannon Lloyd of African Evangelistic Enterprise.

She ties a scarf around the wrists of two people – one the 'victim' and the other the 'perpetrator' to symbolise how they are bound to each other because of what the perpetrator has done. However hard the victim tries to forget what has been done to him, he cannot get away from it. Next, the victim unties his end of the scarf and ties it to a cross, symbolising handing over the hurt and hate to Jesus. In this way the victim can become free of the past. When the perpetrator ties his end to the cross as well, symbolising his repentance and willingness to make amends, he also can be free of the past.

People can only forgive what happened and accept them (the killers) back when the Holy Spirit has brought his transforming love.

Rev Meg Guillebaud

Deborah's story

Deborah's son was shot in 1997.

Although deeply grieving, she prayed for her son's murderer.

A few months later, a young man came to her and confessed to killing her son. 'I killed your son. Take me to the authorities and let them deal with me as they will. I have not slept since I shot him. Every time I lie down I see you praying and I know you are praying for me.'

Deborah said, 'You are no longer an animal but a man taking responsibility for your actions. I do not want to add death to death. But I want you to restore justice by replacing the son you killed. I am asking you to become my son. When you visit me, I will care for you.'

So the man became an adopted son in her household and took on the duties of a son.

Philip's story

Philip was a Hutu and had been brought up by his grandmother to hate the Tutsis. When he had grown up he became a Christian and thought he had put his hatred of Tutsi behind him, but the government propaganda rekindled his feelings and he joined the rebel army, which was called the Interahamwe, and started killing people.

After it was over he was on the run from the police. He began to think about what he had done and a tremendous sense of guilt overwhelmed him.

He allowed the police to catch up with him and confessed to his part in the killings, including some they did not know about. Because of his full confession, he was sentenced to life imprisonment rather than death.

After nine years he was released and ordered to do community service. He was shunned by everyone in the community including the church.

One day he stood up in front of everyone and told them details of what he had done. He was shuddering and weeping with the horror of remembering and because he could not relate to the killer he had once been. The families listened to him and began to understand how truly sorry he was and they too started weeping. They came over to him and hugged him in forgiveness.

The Rev Anasthase Kajugiro, the General Secretary of the Bible Society of Rwanda said, 'Now the perpetrators of the genocide and the genocide victims are working together to show the Rwandan community that God's word is the real foundation of unity and reconciliation.'

●● Think and write ...

1 Choose one of these stories and explain in your own words how the person who had killed found forgiveness.
2 Why do you think Philip stood up and told everyone what he had done?
3 Do you think that Deborah's decision was the right one? Give reasons to support your answer.
4 How can school help people from different backgrounds to learn to live in peace with each other?

●● Discuss

a) What do each of these stories have in common?
b) What are the effects of forgiving someone
  i) on yourself
  ii) on the person you have forgiven?

●● Digging deeper

5 'True repentance is between a person and God and no one else.' Do you agree? Give reasons to support your answer.
6 Many Rwandan men and women think that if they ask for forgiveness, they should not be punished. What would you say to someone who held this view?

25 The work of A Rocha

● ● **Starter**

What does it mean to be a good steward in today's world?

▽ Cover of the A Rocha newsletter.

ISSUE 33 SUMMER 2010   CARING FOR GOD'S WORLD TOGETHER

A ROCHA

2010
International Year
of Biodiversity

'A Rocha' is a Christian organisation that promotes nature conservation. It was founded by Peter and Miranda Harris in 1983 because they believed that one of their tasks, as Christians, was to follow God's command to the first humans and take care of the world as his stewards. They believe that God cares deeply about what happens to the Earth. As it says in Psalm 50, 'Every animal of the forest is mine, and the cattle on the thousand hills. I know every bird on the mountains'.

They hold that the environment is also an issue of justice as it is usually the poor who suffer first when changes occur in the environment.

In actively working for the good of all living things, they aim to persuade humans that they can make the world into a better place. They believe that their work is part of God's great plan to redeem the whole of creation.

The name 'A Rocha' means 'the rock' in Portuguese because the work began in the village of Cruzinha in Portugal. Peter and Miranda established the first field study centre and bird observatory there and the idea caught on. People around the world began to realise that wildlife and its habitats needed to be protected.

One of their tasks, as Christians, is to follow God's command to the first humans to take care of the world as his stewards. Since then, new projects have been started in other parts of Europe, the Middle East, Africa, Asia, America and Australia. Places such as the Aammiq Wetland in Lebanon are now a safe habitat for wildlife thanks to A Rocha.

In the UK in 2002, A Rocha worked with a local council to turn 90 acres of derelict land in west London into the Minet Country Park and Conservation Area. Now it is home to rare birds and butterflies as well as other flora and fauna.

Through its Five Core Commitments, A Rocha maintains its Christian commitment to the environment:

△ Before: derelict land

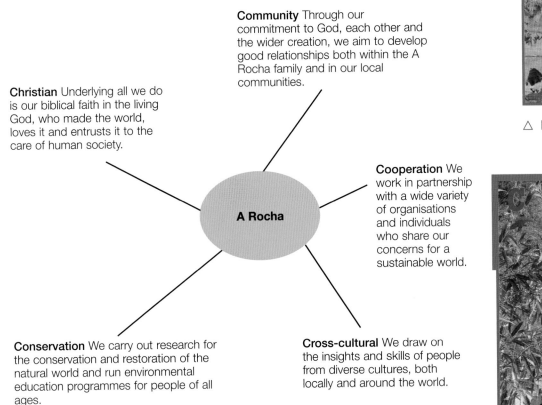

Community Through our commitment to God, each other and the wider creation, we aim to develop good relationships both within the A Rocha family and in our local communities.

Christian Underlying all we do is our biblical faith in the living God, who made the world, loves it and entrusts it to the care of human society.

A Rocha

Cooperation We work in partnership with a wide variety of organisations and individuals who share our concerns for a sustainable world.

Conservation We carry out research for the conservation and restoration of the natural world and run environmental education programmes for people of all ages.

Cross-cultural We draw on the insights and skills of people from diverse cultures, both locally and around the world.

Taken from http://www.arocha.org/int-en/work.html

Local projects are sustained by volunteers who are trained in study centres. Many go on to become environmental professionals and the work goes on. Areas, such as the Arabuko-Sokoke forest on the Kenyan Coast become tourist attractions, bringing in foreign money and creating wealth. In the Arabuko-Sokoke forest, the wealth is used to fund local teenagers through secondary school.

△ After: conservation area

●●● Activity

1 Research the work of A Rocha and present a five-minute talk about its work.

●● Think and write ...

2 How did A Rocha start?
3 What kind of work does it do? Give examples.
4 What are A Rocha's core commitments?

●● Digging deeper

5 How is their work specifically Christian in character?
6 Explain how the work of A Rocha is an example of good stewardship.
7 How can environmental issues also be justice issues?

26 Pacifism and non-violent protest

● ● Starter

Discuss: Do you think there is such a thing as a 'just war'?

Pacifists are people who refuse to fight under any circumstances. They do this because they believe that however just the cause, war is not the solution. Violence is only a short-term solution. The early Christians were pacifists. They refused to fight in the Roman army but, as the Roman Empire began to disintegrate and they were attacked by the barbarians, many became soldiers. It was they who thought of the concept of a just war.

A **just war** has to follow certain guidelines:

● It must be controlled by the government of the country going to war.
● It must have a just cause such as self-defence.
● It must be fought to promote good or prevent evil.
● Peace and justice must be restored as soon as possible.
● War must be the last resort after all other efforts have failed.
● Innocent civilians must not be hurt in the fighting.
● There must be a reasonable chance of success.

The Society of Friends, known as Quakers, are pacifists because they believe that war is against Jesus' teaching on love for our enemies and our neighbours.

Many pacifists were put in prison during the two world wars for refusing to fight. At this time they were accused of cowardice. Many however were prepared to go into the battle zones to bring back the sick and injured. They drove ambulances and were often in direct danger. People who believe it would be wrong to fight in a particular war because it is not a just war are called conscientious objectors.

Arguments in favour of pacifism

● When people are attacked they respond with violence; refusal to fight stops the spiral of violence.
● Many Christians believe that pacifism follows the teaching of Jesus and the Commandments.
● There are better ways of channelling resources instead of using them up to fight wars.

Arguments against pacifism

● Sometimes wars have to be fought to protect the weak. Such wars are called just wars. Loving your neighbour includes defending them from attack.
● Your country may be invaded and people may be forced to fight to defend themselves.

Non-violent protest

● It is closely linked to pacifism and is an alternative to violence.
● Mahatma Gandhi used this idea in his opposition to British rule, as did Martin Luther King in his protests against racism in America, and Desmond Tutu in South Africa.
● Protest may be peaceful, but people can still get killed, for example, in Tiananmen Square, Beijing, in 1989. The students protested against repression in China and when tanks were sent in to dispel them, one student was mown down by a tank and killed.
● Non-violent protests sometimes involve hundreds of people protesting about issues such as nuclear armaments, the environment and animal rights. In 2003 there was a huge non-violent protest against going to war in Iraq. Three million people went to London to protest.
● Non-violent protest can work but it can take a long time.

●● Think and write …

1 What might be your main reason for going to war?
2 What might be your main reason for being a pacifist?
3 Essay practice: 'Christians should not fight in a war.' Do you agree? Give reasons to support your answer.

Was Jesus a pacifist?

The concept of pacifism did not exist in Jesus' day and he never said that war was wrong. Most people think that the enemies referred to in his teaching are personal rather than national enemies. He had at least one Zealot in his team of disciples. Zealots wanted open war against the Romans.

On the other hand, he talked about turning the other cheek, which is the principle of non-retaliation. When he was arrested, he told Peter off for attacking the soldiers.

△ Anti-war protestors in London, 2003.

△ Stretcher bearers in the First World War.

●● Discuss

a) Have you ever been involved in fundraising for a charity?

b) 'People who are injured in the line of duty should not expect special treatment. They are only doing their jobs.' Do you agree with this statement?

People get involved with charities for all sorts of reasons. Often it is because they have had first-hand experience of the difficulties with which the charity concerns itself. For example, if someone you are close to has cancer and Marie Curie nurses have helped them at that difficult time, you might well raise money for that charity. Helping people who are disadvantaged is part of our culture, and also part of the Christian tradition. Many Old Testament prophets such as Isaiah preached about social justice and Jesus taught that we have a duty to love God and to love our neighbour.

Help for Heroes (H4H) is a charity that helps men and women who have been injured while serving their country in the armed services.

How Help for Heros was born

It was founded by Bryn and Emma Parry in October 2007 because they felt profoundly moved by the courage and the plight of soldiers who had suffered life-changing injuries such as the loss of a limb. It all started when the Parrys visited Selly Oak Hospital, Birmingham, in the summer of 2007 where they met some very brave young people who had been badly wounded.

Bryn said afterwards, 'When I walked in, I think that was the moment'. They realised how difficult it must be for active young people to accept their new situations and wanted to do

something to make it possible for them to have real quality of life again. So instead of going home and feeling sorry for them, they were determined to do something positive to help.

'We've just got to do something'

Both Bryn and Emma come from military families and they decided to dedicate their lives to helping these men and women come to terms with their injuries and start new and fulfilling lives. They wanted to raise £8 million to build a new complex at the military rehabilitation centre at Headley Court. They began by organising the 'Big Battlefield Bike Ride', a sponsored ride through France. Three hundred cyclists from all walks of life took part and raised £1.4 million. Eight months later they had the rest of the £8 million they had wanted and something even more important: support and enthusiasm from all round the country. The money poured in and Help for Heroes became a national phenomenon.

Personal sacrifice

Bryn and Emma had to make a decision about their futures because if they were to continue to run the charity, they would have to make sacrifices in their own lives. After leaving the army, Bryn had set up a cartoon business, which he ran with the help of his wife. It was very a successful company but they decided to give it up and devote their time and energies to helping those wounded in battle.

Help for Heroes has a board of trustees. They are businessmen, some of whom have military backgrounds, who donate their expertise and advice in a wide range of areas. The charity's founder patrons are Jeremy and Francie Clarkson, General Sir Richard Dannatt KCB CBE MC and Richard Benyon MP.

Fundraising is done by people all over Britain. At the Great North Road Run on 19 September 2010, £4000 was raised by six-year-old James Corrigan, who ran one mile with his grandfather, Major John Corrigan, a seasoned marathon runner.

Help for Heroes – five key messages

'It's about the blokes': men and women who have been wounded on recent active service.

It does not seek to criticise or be political. All the armed forces are treated equally.

It provides direct, practical support for Britain's wounded.

The money it gets in goes straight out again for help where it is needed. All administration costs are met by selling H4H products.

It's about doing your bit whoever you are and however big or small your contribution is. Every fundraiser is special and can make a difference.

Adapted from www.helpforheroes.org.uk

Here are some of the events that fundraisers take part in:

- carrying a stretcher up the Rock of Gibraltar
- climbing Mount Kilimanjaro
- running through the Brazilian Amazonian rainforest in six days
- rowing across the Atlantic Ocean
- driving from England to Mongolia as part of the Mongol Rally
- running the North Pole marathon – on the frozen Arctic Ocean.

●●● **Activity**

1 Look up the Help for Heroes website and find out more about the work that Bryn and Emma Parry have done to help wounded servicemen and women.
2 In groups, 'set up' a charity for something you are all passionate about. Ask your teacher for a form to help you.
   - Establish your aims.
   - Decide who you might ask to be your patron and write a letter telling them about the charity and why you want them to be a patron.
   - Elect a 'fundraiser' and decide on two or three fundraising events that could be done at your school or where you live.

Essay practice
'A small group of thoughtful, committed people can change the world.'
(Margaret Mead, American anthropologist)
Do you agree? Give reasons to support your answer.

Answering a Common Entrance paper

Before you start

- ☑ Read the instructions on the front page. Your teacher will have gone over what you have to do but remind yourself.
- ☑ Note the time you have:
  40 minutes if you have done coursework;
  60 minutes if you haven't.
- ☑ Note the parts of the paper you have to answer. This will depend on whether you have done coursework or not.
- ☑ Work out the time you will need for each question and leave enough time for the longer ones and for checking your work.

How the marks are awarded

It is very important that you understand that Common Entrance is an entrance examination into your chosen senior school. It is the **senior school for which you are entered who marks your paper** and as senior schools set different standards there is no way in which one can be totally certain how they will mark your paper.

However, the Independent Examinations Board (ISEB) does publish with each paper a marking scheme which is intended to help senior schools mark to a common set of expected answers. Most will use these schemes.

Two-thirds of the available marks are awarded on sections 1 and 2, which this book covers, so it is important you prepare carefully.

Sections 1 and 2 together are divided into four themes. The Old Testament themes are 'God, human nature and covenant' and 'Leaders and prophets'. The New Testament themes are 'Jesus' teaching' and 'Jesus' life, death and resurrection'. You have to answer one question from the Old Testament section and one from the New Testament section. Each question has four parts. The page opposite shows you what you have to do in each part and how the marks are allocated.

How much do I have to write?

Be guided by the marks.

- ☑ The first question carries only two marks so you will not need to write much.
- ☑ The second and third questions are longer and you should be writing a paragraph for each. Your teacher can give you a sheet of guidelines for writing good paragraphs.
- ☑ The fourth question is phrased like an essay question but no more than two or three paragraphs are required.

When you have finished:

- ☑ Proof read your answers.
- ☑ Check for your common mistakes: words you have difficulty spelling, names you get mixed up and so on.
- ☑ Check that you have answered all the correct questions and not left part of one out.
- ☑ If you find that you have left a huge chunk out, write the number of the question at the end of the paper and write the rest of your answer there. Put a note by the question earlier in the test to alert the examiner to the fact that you have written more.

PART	QUESTION TYPE	MARKS AVAILABLE

a

Factual information
2 marks

This question asks for a piece of factual information or a brief definition.

For example: 'Who was Uriah the Hittite?'
'What is a parable?'

Your answers might be:

He was the husband of Bathsheba.

It is a story comparing everyday things with the Kingdom of God

b

Knowledge
6 marks

This part asks you to write a full paragraph. The examiner will be looking for how you organise what you have learnt.

Just because there are 6 marks does not mean you have to make only 6 points. You could make more than that. The key thing is that the facts are relevant. Do not write everything you know about the subject: be selective.

For example: 'Retell the parable that the prophet Nathan told David.'

There are six levels of response.

c

Understanding or interpretation
6 marks

This part asks you to write a full paragraph. The examiner will be looking for how well you understand the passage and how clearly you explain what it means. (When you make a statement try to link it firmly with the relevant part of the text.) Again, there are 6 marks. Try to make three clear, well-explained points.

For example: 'Explain the purpose of Nathan's parable.'

There are six levels of response.

d

Evaluation
7 marks

This part asks you to answer a question usually presented as a quotation with which you can agree or disagree. Your task is to **argue** for or against the quotation using modern examples and references to the Bible, where appropriate. This question carries 7 marks and you will need to write two or three paragraphs. You should make sure you leave yourself enough time for this type of question as it will take you longer than the others.

Although you will probably want to structure your answer into three paragraphs, it does not need to be long. However, this difficult skill is intended to sort out the good and bad candidates. It is also a skill that is much valued by senior schools and is an important part of GCSE Religious Studies.

Your answer is marked according to the six different levels of response, but there are seven marks available. This allows for a more precise analysis of your answer.

For example: 'No one has Peter's faith and determination today.'
Do you agree? Give reasons to support your answer.

Total: 21 marks

Answering the longer questions

Knowledge questions

'Retell the parable that the prophet Nathan told David.' Your answer might be:

There were two men – one rich and one poor and the rich man had many cattle and sheep but the poor man only had one lamb which he treated as a child. One day a visitor arrived at the rich man's house and the rich man didn't want to kill one of his own lambs and took the poor man's lamb.

This is a level 6 answer because it covers all the main points, clearly and accurately.

Understanding or interpretation questions

'What was the purpose of Nathan's parable?' Your answer might be:

Nathan told the parable to try to get David to make a judgement on his own guilt. As David was the king he was the also the 'judge' for Israel and therefore needed to understand his responsibilities. When Nathan had told his story David made his judgement. But he failed to realise that it was referring to his own relationship with Uriah the Hittite - the poor man and his lamb in the parable. So just as the rich man was responsible for taking the poor man's sheep, so David was responsible for the killing of Uriah and he therefore condemned himself.

This is a level 6 answer. Notice how some background information has been used in the second sentence. This is important for interpretation of the rest of the story. Note also how the interpretation works its way step by step through the story so each bit of it is covered.

Evaluation questions

Evaluation questions are intended to be demanding so as to sort out the very good candidates from the rest. They are designed to allow you to bring in contemporary debates about modern issues.

Remember that evaluation questions **also** count for one-third of the marks available, so it is worth getting the technique right to score good marks.

The questions are based on the issues raised by the Biblical passage but you don't always have to refer to the passage to gain high marks.

The following guidelines can help.

- Briefly **explain** the problem.
- Give an argument which supports the question and briefly state its strengths and weaknesses, making sure you give and explain at least one **example**.
- Give an argument which argues **against** the question and briefly state its strengths and weaknesses making sure you give and explain at least one **example**.
- **Conclude** by referring back to the question.

Marking of evaluation questions will depend on the standard each senior school sets. The guidance given to senior schools by ISEB sets six different **levels** of responses and suggested marks.

Level	Mark	Level descriptor
1	1	Gives a **very poor** answer: no essay structure; a very brief answer; a statement with no reasoning; very little reference to the question; poor or irrelevant examples; makes little sense.
2	2	Gives a **basic** answer: a viewpoint is expressed with minimum justification; an example given; some relevance but not a great deal.
3	3	Gives a **broadly satisfactory** answer: some structure or organisation of ideas; lacks clear reasoning; some relevant points; unbalanced; limited examples.
4	4	Gives a **satisfactory** answer: reasonably clear structure and balanced answer; some examples and sound explanation; reasonable expression; one or two relevant points made with reasons.
5	5	Gives a **good** answer: good, clear structure and balanced answer; well-chosen examples with a sound grasp of their meaning; sound assessment of ideas with good reasons.
6	6	Gives a **very good** answer: very good structure; ideas developed in a balanced way; insightful reasons / evaluation; well-chosen and relevant examples.
6	7	Gives an **excellent** answer: excellent structure and balanced answer; sharp reasoning; very good use of language; always focuses on the question; uses well-chosen examples to illustrate the points being made.

For example: 'In the parable of the lost son, the real lessons are to be learnt from the behaviour of the elder son.' Do you agree? Give reasons to support your answer.

Answer

The parable is meant to teach people that God will forgive anyone who is truly sorry for what they have done. The elder son represents the Pharisees who cannot grasp that God loves sinners as well as people who keep the law. The Pharisees thought that God was a judging God but by telling this parable Jesus was trying to get people to understand that worshipping God is simple and that all people needed to do was love God and your neighbour.

I think this parable teaches people a lot about how to worship God. I think the elder son does have a very important part in the parable and many lessons can be learnt from the older son. However, I think that the most important lesson to be learnt is that God loves everybody – even sinners.

So, I don't agree with the statement, but I do believe the elder son does have a very important part in the parable.

Comments

The candidate summarises how they understand the parable in a single sentence. This helps them set out their argument in a good clear way.

Their understanding of the meaning of the parable is helped with a very important piece of interpretation. The candidate therefore contrasts judgement with the Christian teaching on love.

This paragraph follows logically on from the point made in the previous paragraph and now begins to be much more personal.

The point made is a subtle one. The candidate agrees with the question to an *extent*. The more important point is that God loves all including sinners. The candidate could have referred more directly to the younger son, but this is already a full answer and they probably did not have time to write more.

Good use of 'so' to show that this paragraph is the conclusion. The conclusion refers back to the question and makes the candidate's own view very clear.

Glossary

ALTAR A table, often made of stone, used for making sacrifices. In Christian worship an altar is found in a church and used for Communion or Mass.

APARTHEID The separation of black and white people in all areas of life. This used to be the case in South Africa.

ARK OF THE COVENANT The sacred box containing the two tablets of the Law (the Ten Commandments).

ATONEMENT Re-establishment of a right relationship with God.

BAAL A Canaanite god. The Israelites often turned away from God and went back to worshipping Baal, for example at the time of Elijah.

BAPTISM The religious practice of immersion in water. It symbolises turning away from wrong doing, and turning towards God. It is a symbolic washing-away of sin. For Christians it is the moment when they become part of the world-wide Church.

BELIEF A genuine and firmly held opinion.

BLASPHEMY An insult to God's honour. Most commonly associated with using his name in an insulting way. In the New Testament, this could mean speaking against the Temple or claiming to be equal with God.

BLESSED Knowing true happiness as given by God.

CALLING Belief that God has a particular purpose for you in life.

CATHOLIC Can mean two things: firstly the universal Christian Church and secondly the Roman Catholic Church, whose most senior bishop, the Pope, lives in Rome.

CHRIST Literally means 'annointed one'. It is the Greek word for 'Messiah'.

CHRISTIAN The name given to a follower of the teachings of Jesus Christ.

CHURCH The name given to the Christian organisation throughout the world. A church (small c) is a Christian place of worship.

CIRCUMCISION Cutting off the foreskin as an outward sign of the Covenant. Every Jewish boy has this operation when he is eight days old.

COVENANT An agreement entered into by two or more people. Each party will make promises to the other. If one party does not keep his/her side of the agreement, the covenant will be broken. In the Bible it is an agreement between God and his people.

CRUCIFIXION A method of Roman execution by being nailed to a cross. Jesus died this way.

DISCIPLE Someone who follows a teacher and tries to live according to that teaching. Jesus had twelve disciples.

DISCRIMINATION To treat a person or group of people differently from others, either to their advantage or more usually to their disadvantage. Discrimination is usually by race or gender.

EDEN The garden of paradise where everything is perfect (Genesis 2).

EUTHANASIA The act of bringing about an easy death, sometimes called 'mercy killing'.

FAITH Confidence and trust in someone or in God.

FASTING Going without food to enable oneself to become more aware of God.

FORGIVENESS To pardon someone. To restore a relationship with someone who has wronged you.

GOSPEL An old English word meaning 'good news'.

HEAVEN The traditional place where God lives. Also the place where believers go after they die.

HOLY Separate or apart. For example, the Holy of Holies, where the presence of God was believed to stay, was separated from the rest of the Temple by a huge curtain that went from floor to ceiling.

HOSPICE A place where the very ill and dying can go for care and support.

INCARNATION God in human form, in the person of Jesus.

JUSTICE Fair treatment of others.

MESSIAH   The Hebrew word meaning 'annointed one' and used to refer to the king or leader who would be God's servant. Jesus was called the Messiah.

MIRACLE   An act of God which interferes with the laws of nature. Jesus was considered to have had God's power to perform miracles.

MISSIONARY   A person who is called by God and sent to tell people about Jesus Christ/Christianity.

MYTH   A story that has truth in it but no one knows for sure whether it really happened as it is recorded.

NEW TESTAMENT   The second half of the Bible. The word literally means 'new covenant'. It contains the life and teaching of Jesus, and the development of the Early Church.

OLD TESTAMENT   The first half of the Bible. It contains the Law of Moses, the history of the Jewish people and the writings of their prophets.

PARABLE   A story that explains a principle or truth. Jesus used parables to explain the Kingdom of God to the people.

PHARISEE   Jewish religious leaders who believed that by keeping the oral traditions of the Law, they would go to Heaven.

PRAYER   Talking and listening to God.

PREJUDICE   An opinion based on feelings rather than fact.

PRIEST   A person who represents people to God. In the Old Testament the priests carried out sacrifices commanded by God.

PROPHET   A person with a message from God for one or more people.

RABBI   The Hebrew word meaning 'teacher'. Today it means a Jewish leader.

RECONCILIATION   Bringing together people or groups who have something against each other. Reconciliation often starts with forgiveness.

REDEMPTION   Literally means 'buying back' and therefore is the way people are restored to a full relationship with God.

REPENTANCE   Being genuinely sorry for what you have done wrong.

RESURRECTION   Jesus was raised from the dead by God, after three days in the tomb. Christians believe that they also will be raised from the dead to life with God in Heaven.

RIGHTEOUS   Being in a right relationship with God.

SABBATH   Jewish day of rest when God rested after creating the world.

SACRIFICE   Give up something for something of greater value.

SADDUCEE   Member of a Jewish group who denied the resurrection of the dead.

SALVATION   Literally 'healed'. Being healed or saved from the effects of sin and brought into a relationship with God.

SANHEDRIN   The highest court of law in Israel. It was this court that sentenced Jesus to death for blasphemy, before handing him over to Pilate. It was also the court before which Peter and the apostles appeared in Acts 5.

SATAN   The Devil.

SCRIBE   Scribes made and kept copies of the Law and helped interpret the Law.

SIN   Breaking God's Law and therefore being separated from God's love.

SINAI/HOREB   The holy mountain of God.

SINNER   A person who disobeys God's law; an outcast from Jewish society.

SON OF GOD   Jesus had a special relationship with God, whom he called 'Father'. The Gospels record God's voice from Heaven calling Jesus 'my son' both at his baptism and later at his transfiguration.

SON OF MAN   Jesus referred to himself as the Son of Man. By using this title, Jesus identified with human suffering. He was the perfect example of how God's will can be carried out by human beings in this world. The Son of Man would also be God's judge.

SPIRITUAL   Concerned with the spirit, rather than earthly things. For example, thinking about what makes us better people is a spiritual thing to do; planning a weekend out is an earthly activity.

STEWARDSHIP   Looking after things for someone else. For example, we are looking after God's world for future generations.

SYNAGOGUE   Where Jews worship. They are still in use today.

TEMPLE   There was only one Temple and it was in Jerusalem. It was the only place where the Jews offered sacrifices. The Romans destroyed it in AD 70.

TEMPTATION   The desire to do something wrong.

TRANSFIGURATION   Change of appearance.

TRIBE   Each of the twelve Jewish tribes was descended from one of Jacob's sons.

TRINITY   The idea that the Father, Son and Holy Spirit make one God, not three.

UPRIGHT   Honest, loyal, honourable.

WISDOM   Spiritual insight into everyday living. The ability to distinguish right from wrong. Solomon was given this gift by God.

WORSHIP   Giving God reverence, praise and honour.

ZEALOT   A member of a group of freedom fighters who opposed the Roman occupation of their country.

Index

Acknowledgements

Photo credits

Cover © by Dr. He Qi (www.heqigallery.com); **p.4** *tr* © jim – Fotolia, *l* © ussatlantis – Fotolia, *br* © Aurélien Pottier – Fotolia; **p.5** *l* © Design – Fotolia, *tr* © Mona Reeder/Dallas Morning News/Corbis, *br* © Janine Wiedel Photolibrary/Alamy; **p.6** © marcofocus – Fotolia; **p.8** *t* © JULIAN BAUM/SCIENCE PHOTO LIBRARY, *b* © Susan Grenfell; **p.11** *l* © Luiz C. Marigo/Peter Arnold/Still Pictures, *r* © Colin Garratt, Milepost 92 ½/CORBIS; **p.14** Man Being Expelled from the Garden © by Dr. He Qi (www.heqigallery.com); **pp.18, 19, 20 & 21** Images taken from *The Lion Graphic Bible* by Jeff Anderson and Mike Maddox, published by Lion Hudson plc, 2004. Copyright © 2002 Jeff Anderson and Mike Maddox. Used with permission of Lion Hudson plc.; **p.22** © Janine Wiedel Photolibrary/Alamy; **p.24** © akg-images/Erich Lessing; **p.28** © akg-images; **p.29** © Süddeutsche Zeitung Photo/Scherl; **p.34** *t* © The Bigger Picture/Link, *b* © Bettmann/CORBIS; **p.35** © Mayibuye/Link; **p.38** © Nir Alon/Alamy; **p.40** © Bettmann/CORBIS; **p.41** © Bettmann/CORBIS; **p.47** © Joel Stettenheim/CORBIS; **p.50** Images taken from *The Lion Graphic Bible* by Jeff Anderson and Mike Maddox, published by Lion Hudson plc, 2004. Copyright © 2002 Jeff Anderson and Mike Maddox. Used with permission of Lion Hudson plc.; **p.52** © Aaron Horowitz/CORBIS; **p.54** © epa/Corbis; **p.55** © Rex Features; **p.57** Images taken from *The Lion Graphic Bible* by Jeff Anderson and Mike Maddox, published by Lion Hudson plc, 2004. Copyright © 2002 Jeff Anderson and Mike Maddox. Used with permission of Lion Hudson plc.; **p.59** Solomon's Judgement © by Dr. He Qi (www.heqigallery.com); **p.60** *tl* © PETER BROOKER/Rex Features, *tc* © Tim Rooke/Rex Features, *tr* © John Walmsley/eduphotos, *bl* © 2002 Topham/PA/TopFoto, *bc* © PA Wire/Press Association Images, *br* © Brenda Prince/Photofusion; **pp.62 & 63** Images taken from *The Lion Graphic Bible* by Jeff Anderson and Mike Maddox, published by Lion Hudson plc, 2004. Copyright © 2002 Jeff Anderson and Mike Maddox. Used with permission of Lion Hudson plc.; **p.64** Idol of the storm god Baal, from Syria, Bronze Age (c.1350-1250 BC) (bronze and gold)/© Private Collection/Peter Willi/The Bridgeman Art Library; **p.66** © CHRIS PIZZELLO/AP/Press Association Images; **p.67** © Kurt Krieger/Corbis; **p.68** © Noam – Fotolia; **p.75** *l* Courtesy of Oxfam (photo © Greg Williams), *r* © Susan Grenfell; **p.84** © Adrian Brooks/Rex Features; **p.85** © Mary Evans Picture Library/Alamy; **pp.86 & 87** Images taken from *The Lion Graphic Bible* by Jeff Anderson and Mike Maddox, published by Lion Hudson plc, 2004. Copyright © 2002 Jeff Anderson and Mike Maddox. Used with permission of Lion Hudson plc.; **p.88** © Kirill Trifonov – Fotolia; **p.92** Reproduced courtesy of Vie de Jesus Mafa www.jesusmafa.com; **p.93** Christ in the House of Simon the Pharisee, c.1656 (oil on canvas), Champaigne, Philippe de (1602–74)/© Musee des Beaux-Arts, Nantes, France/Giraudon/The Bridgeman Art Library; **p.96** © The Salvation Army; **p.98** © Shai Ginott/CORBIS; **p.100** © The Bible Society; **pp.102 & 103** *t & b* © Mission Aviation Fellowship UK; **p.105** Jesus Calming the Storm © by Dr. He Qi (www.heqigallery.com); **p.106** © Brooklyn Museum/Corbis; **p.108** © AP/Press Association Images; **p.109** © JEAN-PHILIPPE ARLES/Reuters/Corbis; **p.111** © akg-images/Erich Lessing; **p.113** © akg-images/Cameraphoto; **p.116** © Jamie Harron; Papilio/CORBIS; **p.122** © Reuters/CORBIS; **p.123** © Walter Hodges/CORBIS; **p.124** *t* © 2005 Topfoto/PA, *b* © Hugh Rooney; Eye Ubiquitous/CORBIS; **p.125** © PA Archive/Press Association Images; **p.127** © Ian Bruce (Photo: Susan Grenfell); **p.131** *t* © Australian War Memorial, *b* © INTEGRITY PARTNERS/THE KOBAL COLLECTION; **p.134** He Is Risen © by Dr. He Qi (www.heqigallery.com); **p.136** © CHRIS HELGREN/Reuters/Corbis; **p.137** © Baci/CORBIS; **p.138** © Kapoor Baldev/Sygma/CORBIS; **p.139** © JAYANTA SHAW/Reuters/Corbis; **p.140** *t* © St Stephen's Society, Hong Kong, *b* © Earl & Nazima Kowall/CORBIS; **p.142** *t* © 2005 UPPA/TopFoto, *b* Courtesy St Christopher's Hospice (photo © Brian Harris); **pp.144 & 145** © Helen and Douglas House; **p.146** *t* © Gideon Mendel/Corbis, *b* © Elizabeth Grenfell; **pp.150 & 151** *t & b* © A Rocha; **p.153** *l* © Bettmann/CORBIS, *r* © Reuters/CORBIS; **p.154** Logo courtesy of Help 4 Heroes; **p.155** *t* © Stephen Simpson/Rex Features, *b* © 2010 Dave J Hogan/Getty Images.

Written sources

Scripture quotations taken from The Holy Bible, New International Version Anglicised. Copyright © 1979, 1984 by Biblica (formerly, International Bible Society). Used by permission of Hodder & Stoughton Publishers, an Hachette UK company. All rights reserved. 'NIV' is a registered trademark of Biblica. UK trademark number 1448790.

pp.96–97 The Salvation Army, three stories of people helped, adapted from the website, www.salvationarmy.org.uk, by permission; **p.102** Mission Aviation Fellowship, 'The best place to be', adapted from *MAF News*, September–November 2004; **p.123** Father John Dear, extract from the website, www.fatherjohndear.org; **p.130** Ernest Gordon, *Miracle on the River Kwai* (Fount, 1995), © 1995 Zondervan Corporation.

Every effort has been made to trace all copyright holders, but if any have been inadvertently overlooked the Publishers will be pleased to make the necessary arrangements at the first opportunity.